Bamboo Years

By John G Pike

First published by Barny Books

ISBN No: 978.1.906542.13.9

Publishers: Barny Books
                Hough on the Hill
                Grantham
                Lincolnshire
                NG32 2BB

                Tel: 01400 250246
                www.barnybooks.biz

Front Cover:
Illustrated by Roger McKay and shows a depiction from
1941 – 45 of the Pacific Fleet in the South China Sea

Bamboo Years is part of the Once Upon A Wartime Series: No 19

Dedicated

to

my daughters

Jenny & Kate

Acknowledgements:

I would like to thank the following for helping to put this book together:
Jose Spinks for typing it all originally
Mick Bye for reproducing the photos
Roger McKay for designing the cover
Molly Burkett for editing and advice
and
Barny Books publishers

BAMBOO YEARS

It was mid-day, March 1st 1942 some miles south of the equator in the Java Sea. The sea, shifting like sheets of plate-glass in the dazzling equinoxal sun, was strewn with debris and a number of floats to which men clung or huddled knee deep in water on them. The cries of the wounded and burned men drifted across the water but no one spoke, numb with disbelief. The horizon to the north was obscured by brown cordite and black smoke which trailed like a scarf across the sky but the Japanese ships that had sunk the Exeter and her two accompanying destroyers had disappeared after picking up some of the survivors. Tall cumulus clouds were building up over the southern horizon betraying the northern coast of Java but, so incapacitated were we that it could have been a thousand miles away. All afternoon our float rode each swell with a sigh, as brief cats-paws of wind ruffled the otherwise glassy surface. There were calls for water of which there was a small supply in the float. Then someone began to sing, a long forgotten and evocative shanty, "Blow the Wind Southerly".

Night enfolded us all at almost precisely six o'clock. My watch had stopped but we were so close to the equator and the equinox that there was little doubt of the exact time. With it came relief from the burning sun on our bare salt caked skins but, for some, it was to be their last night. Darkness brought the fear of loneliness and death that no amount of encouragement from friends could allay. There was a Yeoman of Signals on the float whom I knew, one of the wardroom pantry stewards with a fearful gash running down the full length of his blackened face and about twenty other men half submerged on the float or in the water clinging to the looped rope that hung over the side. Recollection of that night is confused. Sleep was impossible and the moans and cries of the few wounded seemed, at times, to reach a high pitch only to subside again in a regular rhythm which probably coincided with our own waves of consciousness and semi consciousness.

Dawn came with unpremeditated swiftness and the sun was on us again. Two other floats seemed to have drifted away from us and the yeoman, Wright, suggested we unlashed the few paddles in the float and try and join them by paddling. I remember arguing that we would hardly make any headway with the drag of the men in the water and, in any event, none of us had any energy to spare.

As the morning lengthened, we drifted further away from the other survivors. After some hours, someone shouted, "There's a ship." From my poor vantage point in the middle of the float, I could just make out the dark outline of a destroyer and, at that moment, it did not occur to me that it might be Japanese. My feelings of relief at the thought of succour at hand were suddenly transformed when someone croaked, "It's another bloody Jap." Another voice countered that the ship was American but I knew then that, after the events of yesterday, the ship was hardly likely to be American, nor British, nor Dutch and, as it drew nearer, I noticed its strange high flared bows which meant that it could only be Japanese.

But it did not come for us. After what seemed an interminable interval, I noticed that the ship was moving away and, a few minutes later, we heard the loud sound of the engine room telegraph and the suddenly increased beat of the ship's engines gradually receding until we were left with the silence of the sea under a blazing sun and conflicting thoughts of relief, loneliness, apprehension and fear.

We had now been in the water for almost twenty four hours and our numbers seemed to have diminished. Water was now our main concern. My tongue was beginning to swell and my lips burn. It seemed an eternity but probably only a few hours later when, once again, we sighted a small ship heading straight towards us and, within minutes, it was alongside. It was a small Japanese escort destroyer but, this time, I didn't greatly care. As it lost way, it lowered a rope ladder and scrambling nets over the side and the Japanese sailors standing on the lower deck were shouting to us. We were soon scrambling on to the deck, hauling and lifting the wounded with us.

My first encounter with the Japanese at close quarters came as a shock. They were not the buck toothed, bespectacled runts we had

6

been led to believe but well muscled, lithe men with smooth olive-yellow skin and short cropped dark hair around which some of them wore white cloth bands or red polo caps. As I stood alongside the torpedo tubes clad only in an oil soaked shirt and trousers, my thoughts strayed to the time I had been taken to the circus as a boy to see a particular troupe of Japanese acrobats who performed the most skilful acts of daring with hoops of sharp knives and other feats of incredible agility. I came to learn that this was not unusual as they all seemed to possess a certain Simian agility and always moved fast and purposefully. Their faces were, however, completely expressionless and inscrutable. Even though this may have been their first encounter with the enemy, they betrayed not the slightest curiosity nor interest but went about their business, herding us together with the occasional harsh shout. Although it was hot and humid, I was suddenly chilled by the cold menace dominating the scene.

However, by the standards of our subsequent treatment, the Japanese navy were exemplary in their conduct towards us. They saw that we were given water and, later that night, a meal of rice with slivers of fish and a sour tasting bean curd. The wounded received treatment of an elementary kind – disinfectant sloshed into open wounds – and, when it was found that one of our number, a badly wounded boy seaman, had died in the night, they reduced speed and watched silently as we buried him over the side. It was years later that I learned that the humane behaviour of the Japanese navy persisted until the end of 1943 when, it is alleged, under pressure from the Germans, they besmirched their good record by embarking on a policy of unrestricted warfare against ships and survivors.

Towards evening, the destroyer joined the screen of a large convoy of transport ships heading on a south easterly course. We remained huddled and closely guarded and, as time wore on, the full import of what had happened suddenly overcame us. I was now a prisoner of war and all I had known was lost and the future highly uncertain. As I sat staring at the darkening horizon, the lines of the Ancient Mariner came to me –

> I woke and we were sailing on
> As in a gentle weather
> 'Twas night, calm night, the moon was high;
> The dead men stood together.

But, as I looked at the men around me, I felt my spirits slowly begin to rise. With their oil blackened faces, some clad in nothing but underclothes and blue lifebelts, some wounded and exhausted, they were an unprepossessing sight. But many had that insouciance, that air of prickly corps d'esprit that had always marked the British sailor with a natural haughtiness and distinguished him from the rest. And when they looked back at our captors, it was with a slightly amused, if wary, condescending tolerance implying that we were citizens of another order and, on the whole, rather a superior one. I realised too, that whatever lay in store for us, a long nightmare with a Japanese incubus which none of us, at that moment, could have imagined, it was upon each other that our mutual survival depended. For the first time, I began to understand the self protecting fraternity so carefully nurtured by the Royal Navy – Nelson's ideal – the inspiration of brotherhood which expressed itself not only in comradeship but in grace of conduct.

And thus, we all drew closer – a mental closing of ranks with our minds back to back in the face of an incomprehensible enemy as we embarked upon a different kind of war, an intensely personal one of endurance and suffering and of pitting our wits against an enemy who, for all his cruel, diabolical behaviour, proved to be as humourless as he was gullible.

****

15TH of May 1941, 14.00 hours at Scapa Flow, I joined ship.

I was introduced to the officer responsible for the training of midshipmen and the sub lieutenants of the gunroom. The gunroom officers numbered about twenty-five of which fourteen were midshipmen.

Scapa Flow is in the Orkneys, about a dozen miles from the coast of Scotland across the Pentland Firth. It had been the home of the British Home Fleet since the Great War. It was a sweep of water of some twenty miles ringed by land with strange sounding Norse names, Hoy, Flotta, Hoxa and Switha. It provided a perfect anchorage for a large number of ships even if it had always presented a forlorn and inhospitable appearance to many generations of sailors. The islands are clad in heather and grass with only a few hardy trees. bending leeward in the face of the unremitting wind, inhabited mainly by sea birds and sheep. On that spring day in 1941, it was a place of sombre beauty as the sun shone intermittingly through scudding clouds, bathing the hills of Hoy in soft shadows of green and purple against the sparkling sea.

It seemed such a short time ago that I had passed from H.M.S. Conway and appointed a temporary midshipman, Royal Navy Reserve, at the age of 17. Since then I had attended a course at Greenwich where, in the Painted Hall, probably the grandest room in Europe and the ultimate shrine of Britain's naval glory, Nelson lay in state after Trafalgar. I was awed into adopting manners more becoming to a naval officer after the rough and tumble of Merchant Navy training. My posting to the Prince of Wales was, however, an afterthought on the part of the Admiralty as I was originally posted to the armed merchant cruiser, Rajputana, a former P. and O. liner and manned mostly by men of the Royal Navy Reserve like myself. While preparing to leave with orders to proceed to join the Rajpuntana, I was summoned to the Commander's office to be told my posting had been cancelled and to take a week's leave and report back to Chatham. There was no explanation for this sudden change but, when I read some months later that the Rajputana had been lost with heavy loss of life, I marvelled at the apparent prescience of someone at the Admiralty. It was only after the war that my gratitude to this unknown angel was, in this case, misplaced. The Rajpunata was sunk by U-boat on the 13th of April in the Denmark Strait, a good ten days before I was informed that my posting to her had been cancelled. My posting to the Prince of Wales was, therefore, not based on well laid plans, but merely as another bit of flotsam from the side-wash of war.

The Prince of Wales looked enormous and immensely powerful – one of Churchill's "giants bowed in anxious thought". Upon stepping on to the quarterdeck, the vast expanse of the aft 14 inch gun turret completely filled my horizon. Having only seen a large capital ship from a distance, it is difficult to convey the feeling when I first stepped aboard. Perhaps 'overawed comprehension' conveys my feelings best because I found it difficult to see how I would learn the various parts of this vast ship and fit into its complex organisation, but easily identifiable and thus best remembered was the smell of fuel oil, paint and newly baked bread.

HMS Price of Wales – brand new from the builders yard; Cammel Laird of Birkenhead February 1941 (about to lower her Walrus plane)

The Prince of Wales was brand new, only commissioned four months previously. It belonged to a new class of battleship, the King George V class. It was fitted with ten fourteen-inch guns, a radical departure from the eight or nine fifteen or sixteen inch guns traditionally fitted to British battleships. The fourteen inch guns were of an advanced design with a range of over 20 miles and a high rate of fire, two shells per gun per minute. The secondary armament was also of an advanced design of four twin 5.25 inch turrets mounted on each side of the main deck. This total of sixteen 5.25 inch guns had a highly sophisticated control system and were said to be the last word in anti-aircraft armament which, in retrospect, now seems to have been rather a hollow boast. She also carried six sets of eight barrelled 2-pounder pom-poms, sometimes known as Chicago pianos, a 44mm Bofors gun and a large number of 20mm Oerlikon light machine cannons. The ship was commanded by Captain J.C. Leach, a tall, broad shouldered man who had, at one time, been tennis champion of the Navy. It carried over 100 officers and 1,500 men from the Devonport depot. Most of the midshipmen were ex-Dartmouth regular R.N. although there were a number of RNR midshipmen like myself in the gunroom. It was soon established that I was the youngest midshipman and the most junior by date of appointment.

We were up early every morning to attend signals instruction on the flag deck before breakfast, a whole morning instruction in navigation by the 'Schoolie', the Instructor Lieutenant, followed by watch keeping as Midshipman of the Watch on the quarterdeck or in charge of one of the ship's boats which seemed to be called away without interruption throughout the remainder of the day for duty visits to other ships or the dockyard. For the first week, I was also included in a bewildering series of tours to other parts of the ship, given the task of 'tanky', appointed to assist the Navigating officer and then spend what spare time I had with the Yeoman in the chart room correcting charts. When it was discovered that I possessed a good legible hand, (thanks to a certain Miss Pym), I was also given the job of copying the deck log book into the fair or permanent log.

Although we fared better than most in wartime Britain, the food served in the gunroom was indifferent and seemed to consist mostly of powdered egg, soya links and tinned tomatoes (generally known as train smash), grey, unappetising dehydrated potatoes, cod and tough beef and mutton for which we all paid a mess bill of £9 a month. The bread and bacon was always good and my youthful appetite was invariably assuaged with copious draughts of strong tea and bread and jam at afternoon tea. As midshipmen, we were also allowed a small wine bill but were restricted to beer or wine.

This daily routine of initiation to both gunroom and ship went on for nearly a week when we all reacted to a small but significant change in the ship's steady routine. The fleet had been brought to short notice for steam. Across the Flow, tell-tale signs that other ships were being readied for steam were evident. The Hood, the largest ship in the Royal Navy and the King George V, our sister ship and flagship of the Admiral, Sir John Tovey, Commander in Chief, Home Fleet and a host of cruisers and destroyers all betrayed signs of activity with wisps of smoke rising in the shimmer of heat from their funnels. Adding to this bustle, the aircraft carrier, Victorious, returned from exercises during the afternoon.

Later that evening, the ship's company were mustered on the quarterdeck and addressed by the Captain. It was with a sense of eager excitement amid rumours and buzzes that the ship's company fell silent when he began to speak from the top of the after-turret on that warm spring evening. He thanked everyone for their hard work during the last few months and spoke cryptically of trials to come during which, he felt sure, we would acquit ourselves well.

Dinner that night was well remembered, less formal than other dinners spent in harbour. We all felt a quickening of the senses and a cheerful camaraderie which came to precede all our sailings. Some of the more senior midshipmen even spoke to me for the first time and I took my first steps to becoming an acceptable member of the gunroom. Talk was incessant. Opinions and theories as to our destination were as numerous as they were bizarre. These ranged from sailing to meeting the German fleet in a Jutland type, once and for all, decisive battle to showing the flag in America. There were, however, more experienced voices who opined that the ship was far from ready to take part in a major operation, far less actual battle.

There were still dockyard artificers on board trying to rectify persistent faults in two of the main armament turrets. Depressing too was the revelation that many of the ship's company were 'skates', unruly, troublesome ratings.

22nd May. At 00.20 hours the Prince of Wales weighed and proceeded in company with the Hood flying the flag of Vice-Admiral Holland through Hoxa Gate between Flotta and Ronaldsay Islands. Outside the Flow in Pentland Firth, the battle squadron was joined by six destroyers, three A class and three E class who took station as an anti submarine screen ahead and about........

It had been raining and a low mist had settled when we weighed, turned on our engines, formed line ahead and followed the Hood through the Hoxa Gate to the open sea of the Firth. Viewed from the compass platform, the long, graceful silhouette of the Hood gradually transformed into a broad squat shape as she turned ahead of us. A light began to blink out a signal from her bridge. In the years ahead I came to remember this poignant moment when all save three of the 1,500 men on the Hood had already had their last look at land and only those at the station above deck were seeing the low, dark, mist-shrouded islands of the Orkneys for the last time. But, at that moment, such thoughts were far from my mind as I stood in almost incomprehension as understudy to the Midshipman of the watch who was answering the telephone, writing up the deck log and seemingly coping with a hundred small tasks. The platform was now crowded with the Captain, the Navigating Officer, the Chief Yeoman of the Signals and Officer of the Watch who was hugging the gyro repeater compass and giving frequent changes in engine revolutions and course to the wheelhouse below at the bidding of the Navigation Officer. Everyone spoke in a quiet undertone and I marvelled at the complete lack of fuss and the apparent ease at which a 35000-ton battleship could be handled in confined waters. My thoughts however were soon interrupted by the Midshipman of the Watch whispering in my ear to get the ky organised which meant I was to supervise the making of cocoa for everyone. As the Prince of Wales cleared the Flow, I found myself grappling with the mysteries of making a rather unique naval cocoa with one of the messengers in a small space behind the bridge but happily so for I imagined that even the Captain standing immobile on the port side, probably made cocoa for his betters in the Battle of Jutland.

We awoke next morning to a rising sea and wind from the north with the Hood ahead of us fine on the port bow about four cables [800 yards] and churning a broad and confused wake. The sun was already well up although it had only set well past midnight. In these latitudes in late May, it is never dark, merely a long twilight between sunset and sunrise, to the consternation of our circadian rhythm. The fleet maintained double British summer time, two hours ahead of Greenwich time. The disparity between the ship's clock and times of sunrise and sunset gradually increased as we steamed westwards to a point where it was almost impossible to tell the time by the position of the sun or twilight.

Speculation was rife throughout the day as the ship's guns were exercised in range and inclination, the radar sets calibrated and a damage control exercise carried out. I was told that my action station would not now be on the bridge as had earlier been ordered but as a supernumerary midshipman to assist on the air defence position, an exposed position rather like the eagle's eyrie high above and to the rear of the bridge. I spent the afternoon there with the wind whistling around and above us and through the array of halyards and stays, being initiated into the complexities of the innumerable telephones and headsets along which orders were passed between the pilot, the secondary armament, the defence position and the directors. At 6p.m. with the sun still high in the sky, I went on watch in the air defence position. The ship had gone to defence stations which meant that half the ship's armament was now manned and the watches divided into two instead of three as in the case of normal cruising. This also meant watch and watch about or four hours on and four hours off with little time to do anything between except snatch some sleep. Everything I had learned that afternoon had clouded and I was

14

required to go through the simple routine again by one of the officers.

Soon after being relieved at 8 o'clock and upon making my way to the gunroom, the ship changed course to the northward and increased speed. I remained on deck for a while and watched an escorting destroyer on our starboard beam pitch into the sea and rear skywards in a drunken roll as the sea cascaded over it and the waves roller coasted beneath her whilst the wind drove heavy spray across the decks of both the Hood and the Prince of Wales. After I had sat down to a watch-keeper's supper in the gunroom, it was broadcast that we could expect to be in action with heavy German units before the night was out. We soon learned from that mysterious network by which news spread throughout the ship that one of these was the Bismarck, the largest and newest battleship of the German fleet.

Soon afterwards, we all clustered in the chest-flat to change into action clothing which included a mandatory change into clean underclothes, a precaution to prevent wounds becoming infected. After changing, we made our way to the cinema flat where we were issued with white gauntlets reaching to our elbows and balaclava type hoods with a mantle which covered our shoulders. All loose material in the gunroom, curtains, pictures and all breakables were removed and stowed away giving the gunroom a stripped bare appearance which would soon be used as a damage control station. Elsewhere in the ship preparations for action were being carried out. The wardroom was converted into an emergency casualty station. The Warrant Officers' mess and officers' cabins were stripped and additional watertight doors and hatches closed. Accompanying this quiet, purposeful activity was a pitching vibration at near maximum speed and sulphur fumes which were being drawn into the ship's ventilating system causing the eyes to smart and the tongue to become furry and foul.

There was little time for reflection in the short time left to us before going to action stations. Even though I was a newcomer to both the Navy and the sea, I could not draw upon the experience of the other midshipmen as none, save one or two of the senior ones, had seen action before. A sub-Lieutenant had been at sea since the beginning of the war. His experience had been weeks and months on the Northern patrol or at Scapa Flow. He often remarked that going on leave to London was a highly dangerous occupation compared to the war. Whatever our private thoughts were, we kept them to ourselves behind a screen of inane jokes told in youthful, high-pitched voices betraying our nervousness, our increased adrenalin fed quickening of the blood and a heightening of the senses.

At 22.00 hours hands closed up to action stations and I made my way to the Air Defence position. Before the sound of the alarm rattlers and the bugle's urgent, 'doh soh-soh, doh soh-soh' calling all hands to action had died away, men were on the move and those already at their defence watch stations began to test communications. They moved along to their quarters silently although there was some confusion on one main ladder-way where groups moving in opposite directions collided with each other. I can remember thinking how badly organised that was but it was, in retrospect, a symptom of a ship not yet fully worked up with an inexperienced crew. It was cold on the air defence position. Men were testing headsets and phones as I went to my corner. I had memorised the few lines of communication which had become my responsibility. In the late evening light, even though our clocks maintained it was two hours short of midnight, we looked slightly absurd wrapped up warmly in sweaters, duffle coats, lifebelts and anti-flash gear which made us all look like a colony of comic penguins.

The shadows lengthened as we stood silently watching the heaving sea and the Hood, now fine to our port bow, while we pounded our way on a west nor-westerly course at 27 knots. The wind howled through the halyards and while the vibration kept up a steady frisson through us, our eyes swept the northern horizon expecting to see the Bismarck emerging from the late evening haze. As the hours passed, a sense of anti-climax slowly began to overtake us. The transparent insincerity of our smiles to each other betrayed an inner tension and fear alternating with periods of elation. I was cold and tired. My eyes smarted and I felt let down after a long day of rising tension and suppressed excitement. Shortly after midnight, there was a sudden flurry of signals from the Hood, Blue Pennant

16

Four Five, ordering a 45 degree turn to starboard and, as the hoist came fluttering down, we followed her on to a course roughly north west. This was soon followed by another signal hoist – George [G] two five indicating a new reduced speed of 25 knots. With only an imperceptible lessening of the vibration frequency as the ship reduced speed, we were all, nevertheless, instantly alert with a sudden renewed purpose behind our sweeps of the horizon which had, earlier, become somewhat lethargic as the hours passed.

Shortly afterwards, the Captain broadcast to the ship's company saying that we had altered course to close the Bismarck and the Prince Eugen, her accompanying cruiser, on a reciprocal course and that the Suffolk and the Norfolk were shadowing them some ninety miles to the northward and we could expect to make contact at about 1.40 hours. Almost immediately battle ensigns were hoisted, huge white ensigns at the fore and main masts. There was another flurry of signals from Hood's yardarm, blue pennant one-five indicating a 15 degree turn to starboard which brought us on to a course almost due north.

As the hours passed and sunshine gave way to misty twilight, the northern hemisphere remained empty and, once again, we felt let down with a sense of anti-climax – the Bismarck had eluded us. At about 2 a.m., with clouds now darkening the sky and in decreasing visibility, the battle squadron turned abruptly to the south east and this was taken as confirmation that the Bismarck and her consort had indeed slipped past us and, instead of racing towards her, we were following in her wake. We then heard that the Suffolk had lost contact and we were now steering on a converging course on the enemy's supposed track but, an hour later, we were informed that the Suffolk had regained contact and we now altered course a few degrees to starboard to bring us on an interception course.

The news that the Bismarck had been relocated required yet another mental adjustment but this time we felt sure that action was imminent. At 4a.m. we were told that the enemy squadron was less than 20 miles away to starboard and, at our present course and speed, we would probably intercept within two hours and, as if to underline this, there was a sudden increase in vibration as we increased speed to 28 knots.

As the minutes slipped away, I looked for'ard on the port side past the bridge to watch the reassuring sight of the Hood churning out a huge, broad wake as she forged on at almost full speed, her large forward battle ensign slightly obscured by funnel haze. Then the captain broadcast once again saying we could expect to be in action within a quarter of an hour. This was followed by an address from the Chaplain who read that splendid prayer of Sir Jacob Astley before Edgehill, 'O Lord, thou knows how busy we must be today: if we forget thee, do not forget us. Amen'

In the pink glow of a cold dawn slowly replacing the gloom of a deep twilight all eyes strained towards starboard. No one spoke and all that could be heard was the roar of the exhaust from the foremost funnel just abaft our position, the sea and the wind. Here and there were nervous coughs from men staring intently to the west, some almost crouching behind the parapet and wind deflector in an instinctive reaction to the enemy's imminent appearance.

At 5.30 a.m. on the 24th of May, the Bismarck and Prince Eugen were sighted low on the horizon at about Green 45 and steering a converging course.

"Enemy in sight," came the urgent, high-pitched cry of the lookout high in the crow's nest and, with immediate response, the director began to turn to starboard followed by the main armament. For a short while nothing could be seen but gradually the masts and superstructure of two ships appeared out of the horizon and, within another short space of minutes, we saw the entire ships themselves. From our signal yardarm flew flag N – a yellow and blue triangular flag signifying 'enemy in sight' followed by three numeral flags indicating the bearing. The range at that time was about 17 miles but the enemy ships looked to be much closer, like a pair of large, squat powerful and menacing grey wolves. I stood there frozen. I will always remember the tingling sensation crawling up the back of my neck as we waited. Our guns were now trained towards the enemy, all moving slightly in adjustment with each roll and pitch of the ship as though sniffing the air, searching for prey. We then turned again to starboard to bring the enemy ships fine on our starboard bow. By turning to starboard we undoubtedly presented a smaller target but, at the same time, it would prevent us from using our after main armament. It also brought the enemy ships across our bows which would allow them to bring all their guns to bear and achieve a classic battle manoeuvre, known as crossing the tee. As the seconds ticked away and neither side had opened fire, we stared hypnotised as the squadrons raced towards each other like two pairs of jousting knights sizing up each other. A seaman next to me muttered, "I think we're going to ram them." Another answered, "Out fenders, we're going alongside." I found I couldn't utter a word.

On the Hood, the red and white flag 5 – the signal to open fire – remained agonizingly at the hoist while this silent march of the giant adversaries went on as though each was daring the other to fire first. Then, as flag 5 was brought down, the executive signal, the Hood opened fire with her forward main armament. There was a huge flare with ginger brown-black cordite smoke thrown forward followed a few seconds later by an ear shattering blast reverberating across the waves. Almost immediately, the ding-ding of the fire gong from our own director came and we, too, opened fire.

Suddenly the sky was filled with a bright orange flash and an ear shattering roar and blast. Nothing had prepared me for this massive assault on my senses which completely subdued me with a concussive blow expelling the air from my lungs. As the smoke cleared, I tried to see the enemy ships but, from my station on the port side, I could not see anything. Someone shouted, 'She's fired,' and then came the sound of our fire gong and a flash and a concussive roar as we fired again. Now a new sound filled the air, a strange wailing, wuffing sound rapidly increasing in intensity followed by great, towering, blackish-white fountains of water rising from the sea just astern of the Hood. Salvo after salvo now followed as we raced towards the Bismarck and the Prince Eugen. Then we ourselves were drenched with water as one of Bismarck's shells reared up out of the water close to our starboard side. There was also another new sound as high explosive shells, probably from the Prince Eugen, burst overhead with resounding cracks, showering shrapnel over the ship and causing the sea to boil around us as the fragments hit the water.

As each salvo was fired from our forward guns, I came to fear the terrible shock wave more than anything the enemy could do and hoped, rather absurdly, that everyone would stop firing. Those fragments of minutes between the sound of the fire gong and the blast of guns were never constant. Sometimes the blast followed almost immediately but, on other occasions, it seemed an eternity as we all held our breath, clenched our teeth and put our fingers in our ears. There was no distraction of urgent tasks to perform. There was nothing for us on the air defence position to do except pass information from the secondary directors to the 5.25 guns which remained silent and out of range.

One of the last pictures of the Hood, *taken from the Prince of Wales*

After some time, I looked ahead and saw that the Hood seemed shrouded in smoke with flames leaping upward from the boat-deck which I took to be from her guns. But, as I stared, I realised that the Hood was on fire amid-ship and we moved to the port side to watch. Then, almost as if we were watching a slow motion film, the Hood seemed to move sideways and buckle slightly as a vast tower of pale red flame and a whitish-yellow smoke rose to a vast height,

20

spreading out like a mushroom at the top. At the base of this towering growth of smoke, there was a fierce, pulsating flame like a gigantic blow torch with brilliant orange flashes of flame cascading out in all directions now accompanied by a roaring sound.

Simultaneously, there were whole parts of the ship sailing through the air and, even more incredible, was the sight of the after structure and the two after main turrets sliding sideways, suddenly collapsing as if they were made of cardboard and sliding into the sea. At that moment, both ships were turning to port, presumably to bring our armaments to bear and it seemed to me that we were in imminent danger of running right over the disintegrating Hood. But the captain's reactions were faster than my thoughts as we were already turning to starboard under full rudder, bringing the vast pall of smoke now hiding the remains of the Hood to our port side. We raced past continuing to fire salvo after salvo. I was barely conscious of this as I watched the Hood rapidly dismember, her whole fore-end now rising out of the water to an angle of about 45 degrees and sliding into the sea. And there was nothing; no men, no wreckage, nothing except a large area of disturbed water and a pall of rapidly receding smoke.

At that moment we were jerked back from our horrified gaze by the wailing-wuffing sound as yet another approaching salvo and both enemy ships shifted their target to us. In the fraction of a split second before we were engulfed in a massive shock wave of tearing metal and blast, I saw the Bismarck, now on our starboard beam, with our last salvo rising in white columns of water along her port side. I was then slammed against a bulkhead, my head exploding and a high pitched singing in my ears, then nothing else as my world collapsed in a jarring roar.

I regained consciousness some time later with a light shining in my eyes, a strong antiseptic smell and the face of a Surgeon-lieutenant looking at me. He nodded and I drifted back to sleep again unaware that I was drugged with morphine. Later on, I felt as if I was reliving the events of that morning again as the ship shuddered from the blast of a main armament broad-side, slowly realising that I was awake and the blast from the guns overhead was very real. We were

21

in action again. I looked at my watch. It was 6.30. I had no idea whether it was morning or evening. The firing went on for about ten minutes as I counted ten salvoes. I felt no pain. I was comfortably drowsy and slipped off to sleep again until some hours later when I was woken again by two more salvoes. This time I remained awake. I was suddenly alert and very hungry. I had not even eaten the chocolate I had taken to my action station.

Presently a sick bay attendant came and told me that I had not been wounded but had been concussed by a blow to the back of my head. It seemed that I had had a lucky escape as there had been a number killed and wounded on the bridge superstructure. He said that enemy fire had damaged other parts of the ship but the direct hit on the superstructure had been the most serious. He gave me some hot soup and a delicious Cornish pastie [a tiddley oggie].

I was moved from the sick bay to an officer's cabin the next day and told to rest for twenty four hours. I was besieged by a raging head-ache and only vaguely remember visits from the Surgeon-lieutenant and two of the other midshipmen. They told me that, along with the Norfolk, we had been pursuing the Bismarck southwards, had engaged her in two brief skirmishes and were now being detached to Iceland to refuel. They added that the Prince of Wales had been hit seven times and had taken on a lot of water aft. Thirteen men had been buried at sea including two midshipmen. One of them was Linck who had initiated me as we had left Scapa Flow. I reflected on his death with sorrow and, at the same time, offered a prayer of thanks for my own survival.

I returned to the gunroom the next day, May 26th but was excused duties. The weather had turned cold and cloudy with brief flurries of snow. It seemed that the Bismarck had managed to get clear away and was headed for France with the British navy in pursuit. We all felt it was only a matter of time before she would be sunk and that the operation had been dogged by sheer bad luck. The loss of the Hood and the manner of her sinking was still exerting powerful emotions of shock and disbelief. I could not rid myself of the thought of the sudden death of 1,600 men at the hands of the two most elemental forces of nature – fire and water. My thoughts kept wondering what it must have been like below where, without warning, bulkheads would buckle or flash and flame would sear everything in its path, trapping and killing everyone.

Later, I was sent for by the nurse who wanted to know how I was feeling and then escorted me to the Captain who had asked to see me. Captain Leach was in his sea cabin. He was known to one and all as 'Trunky' because of his prominent nose. He looked tired and drawn. He jollied me out of my depressed state. In the months to come, I learned more of our Captain who was universally popular and regarded with affection by officers and men alike. He was devoid of pomposity and considerate and fair with all ranks, particularly the young.

We reached Havalfjord in Iceland in the early hours of Tuesday, 27th of May and work started immediately to repair the damage to the ship. The bridge, radar office, the aircraft crane and the starboard secondary director had all been damaged and one of Bismarck's projectiles had hit the ship below the water line letting in 400 tons of water. Another 8 inch shell had entered the shell handling room but failed to explode.

Later that afternoon, it was broadcast to the ship that the Bismarck had been sunk 200 miles south west of Ireland by units of the Home Fleet.

We were jubilant at the news and, for the first time, the heavy depression which had stayed with us since the sinking of the Hood was lifted although we all felt disappointed at not being in at the kill ourselves. We also felt that the Prince of Wales would for ever be linked with the disaster that had befallen the Hood and this was confirmed the next day when the Kenya, a six inch gun Colony Class cruiser, secured alongside. We invited some of the midshipmen over and they made it clear that they thought we had shown a lack of fighting spirit after the sinking of the Hood by withdrawing. It was true that our fourteen inch guns out ranged those of the Bismarck and we could have opened fire sooner but we were acting under the orders of Admiral Holland in the Hood who seemed reluctant to do so until the range had closed. It is also true that the combined fire power of ourselves and the Hood exceeded that of the two German ships who carried eight fifteen-inch and eight eight-inch guns respectively to our combined total of eighteen fourteen-inch and fifteen-inch guns. A lot was written about the sinking of the Hood in later years and the common verdict is that Admiral Holland made the mistake of approaching the Bismarck and Prince Eugen at too fine an angle thus reducing the number of guns that could be brought to bear and by not allowing the Prince of Wales to use her modern fifteen-inch guns at an extreme range. He was undoubtedly anxious to present as small a target as possible and get close to the enemy to avoid being hit with a plunging projectile on the Hood's lightly armoured upper deck and, in doing so, probably hoped to offset this disadvantage by meeting Bismarck's projectiles on a flatter trajectory. As it happened, it was this type of high, plunging salvo that destroyed the Hood in a few minutes.

We felt we were being unfairly held to blame in some way for the sinking of the Hood for failing to immediately avenge her sinking.

The damage sustained by the Prince of Wales was extensive, extending from the superstructure to just above the starboard screw. Out of seven hits, only three detonated. The two fifteen-inch which struck the bridge and the lower part of the high angle director support near the air defence position did not detonate either. An unexploded 15 inch shell was found in the starboard side of the after boiler room well below water level after we had reached port much to everyone's surprise.

Many of the gunroom officers went off on leave but this was not granted to me. I set about a period of study and exploration of the ship. I had always had an interest in navigation and felt drawn to the engine rooms with their vast turbines, pipes, valves and instruments. I was fascinated by this huge concentration of controlled power which could be finely adjusted to allow the ship to keep a precise station by merely varying the speed by as little as one revolution a minute.

****

After extensive repairs, the Prince of Wales returned to Scapa Flow in July 1941 and commenced a new series of exercises at sea. These went on unremittingly for months, throw off shoots at other ships, battle practice, target shooting, range and inclination, anti-aircraft range firing, anti-aircraft close range firing, night encounter, damage control and radar calibration exercises. During the repair period, a number of alterations to the ship were made and, in place of the air defence position, there was now a circular glassed in structure which housed the new surface radar set. The air defence position was now set lower down and in a more accessible position.

After divine service on Sunday, August 3rd, preparations for sea began and we were informed that we would put to sea in twenty-four hours.

It rained in a steady drizzle throughout the next day. Evening came and it seemed to many of us that we were being held ready for another interception of a German battleship trying to break out into the Atlantic. We knew that the Scharnhorst and the Gneisenau were formidable, modern battleships and we speculated that the Germans, emboldened by their near success with the Bismarck, might well try again with a heavier force. We were not to know that these two particular ships along with the Prince Eugen were bottled up in Brest. But nothing prepared us for the sudden arrival alongside us of the Oribi that evening. A gangway between the ships was rigged and no less a personage than Mr Winston Churchill came aboard. He was dressed in black and wore his well-known Trinity cap. He was soon followed by the First Sea Lord, Sir Dudley Pound, General Sir John Dill and an unfamiliar Air Marshall. Following behind them was a comet tail of mainly naval captains and army colonels together with a long retinue of staff and baggage.

The Prince of Wales slipped her moorings at 11p.m. in persistent drizzle and proceeded through the Hoxa Gate turning westward in the Pentland Firth where we were joined by three destroyers. The weather deteriorated soon after clearing the shelter of the land and the Prince of Wales ploughed into heavy seas with the destroyers struggling hard to keep station. At times, it seemed as if they would disappear altogether, the sea almost enveloping their small superstructures only to cascade aft as the bows reared into the air completely submerging their sterns.

The ship's routine had been considerably tightened and for those of us with watch-keeping stations on or near the bridge, we seemed to be perpetually at attention as innumerable senior staff officers haunted the various ladders and passageways with marine sentries at every door. The prime minister had found the captain's day cabin in the stern of the ship far too uncomfortable with excessive vibration of the screws beneath. He had himself moved to the admiral's sea cabin below the compass platform. On going off watch one evening, I descended the ladder from the bridge and, on running round a corner into a howling wind, I came face to face with him. He was staring gloomily at the wild sea, his hands deep in his black bridge coat and his cap set squarely on his head. He looked at me quizzically and then said, "How old are you, boy?" I told him and he merely nodded and gave an encouraging smile. A civilian approached him at that instant and glared at me whereupon I took myself off.

The weather deteriorated on the second day of our voyage with an increasing sea from the north-west. The destroyers were unable to keep up with us at our speed of 20 knots. Rather than reduce speed, they were detached and soon lost in the spume and spray astern as they made for Scapa Flow.

We saw a film show in the cinema flat that evening which Churchill and some of the senior staff attended. The film featured Vivien Leigh as Lady Hamilton and Laurence Olivier. When it ended, the Prime Minister stood up and addressed us all. He spoke of the events portrayed on the screen and drew a parallel to those in which we too were taking part. In that dimmed cinema flat this magnificent, puckish, incorrigible imperialist stood before us like some actor in an imperial theatre, our eager youthful faces smiling back in agreement with his words. He spoke with dramatic rhetoric verging on hyperbole and confirmed that we were a very special people. At that moment, as we voyaged silently and darkened across the North Atlantic, making frequent alterations of course to avoid German U boats, we nevertheless believed in him. We were later to have good cause to wryly contemplate Churchill's words of implied invincibility before the year was out. A number of us soon came to replace these shibboleths for a more enduring, more personal faith.

Afterwards, in the gunroom and away from the spell of Churchill, we reverted to irreverent, ribald debate. Although Churchill seemed to be genuinely pleased and relaxed in the company of the navy, I learned much later that he sneered that the navy's ancient traditions consisted only of sodomy, rum and the lash. He was right, for the navy's legend is largely an amalgam of sensual emotionalism, carnal ebullience and ruthless absolutism. All these elements, thickly overlaid with sheer swank and experience compose the style of the Royal Navy which has always been its most potent asset - this style whereby the experience of centuries had been distilled of its impurities with only the pure spirit remaining. The very age of this experience also made for mystery giving the navy an arcane manner unattainable to outsiders who watched with perplexity the strange rituals of tradition and particularly those surrounding the name of Nelson.

The English seaman was held in low esteem in the 16th century. Until the 19th century discipline was vicious, the food inedible, conditions were squalid and the lives of many seamen consisted of a hopeless round of desertion, recapture and flogging. The ports at which the navy made its home were the toughest and most notorious in the world. It was Nelson who changed much of this raffish image and his successes transformed the Navy's reputation and established Britain's supremacy on the sea. He opened the way to imperial glory and established the legend of the Royal Navy.

As we progressed westwards, it became clear to all of us that we were proceeding direct to America. There was no doubt in our minds that a meeting between Churchill and the President of the United States was in the offing. This stimulated a continuing debate in the gunroom. The more well informed said that America was a neutral country and Mr Roosevelt would not dare to flaunt the strong isolationist sentiment of his country. We eventually decided that Canada was our destination but we were not sure for what purpose.

There were continual alterations of course on August the 7th as signals had been received on the probable position of U boats. A new destroyer escort joined us in moderating weather. On the 9th of August, Cape Rush on the south-eastern corner of Newfoundland was sighted. Shortly afterwards we rounded the Cape and steered close inshore to Placentia Bay, a large south facing sound which almost divided Newfoundland in two.

As we entered the bay which was surrounded by bare, dark green hills, we noted a number of American ships at anchor. In the centre of the bay was the S.S.Augusta flanked by the cruiser, Tuscaloosa and directly ahead lay the battleship Arkansas with her strange but distinctive trellis work bridge structure rising like a miniature Eiffel Tower. Soon after anchoring, the Prime Minister and his party disembarked and headed towards the Augusta. Some time later we were told that the Prime Minister was conducting a series of talks with Mr Roosevelt, the American President. We did not know it then but this meeting was to forge the Atlantic Charter, a declaration of common aims between Britain and the United States. History shows us that the Prime Minister was forced to compromise his imperialist principles by agreeing to a phrase inserted by Mr Roosevelt which specifically recognised 'the right of all people to choose the form of government under which they live'. This was intended to refer to the British Empire in particular.

This meeting was seen by us to be a preliminary step towards a declaration of war against Germany by America. We, somewhat naively, expected this to happen immediately. None of us could have imagined the turn of fate, the circumstances which would bring them into the war and which would take us towards our own destruction on the other side of the world.

President Roosevelt came aboard the Prince of Wales on the following day with a large staff of several hundred officers and men of the United States Navy and Marines to attend Divine Service. For the first time, we saw how badly crippled he was from polio. He had to be supported by two officers, one of whom was his own son. He took his place with Churchill in seats before the pulpit draped with the Union Jack and the Stars and Stripes. Everyone sang Onward

Christian Soldiers and other suitable hymns that seemed as familiar to the Americans as they were to us.

HMS Prince of Wales at Placentia Bay Newfoundland, during the Atlantic Charter Meeting

We were much taken by the Americans. They were the first I had ever met. A group of ensigns and lieutenants were later asked to share a drink with us in the gunroom, an invitation they accepted with puzzling alacrity until we discovered that American ships were dry. No alcoholic drink was carried on their ships. The ensigns were our equivalent in rank and they were puzzled to find midshipmen at sea. In the United States, midshipmen were still at what they called a Naval Academy, the equivalent of our cadets. They were soon pressing us for details of our encounter with the Bismarck. They scrupulously tried to maintain a neutral stance and avoided any criticism of the Germans. What impressed us most was the apparent good health and vigour – tanned faces under short cropped hair, an easy familiarity which contracted strongly with our rather pink to pasty white faces and diffident reserved manner. By a strange coincidence, I was to meet one of these ensigns a year later but under very different circumstances.

29

One day, boatloads of small white boxes containing cigarettes and fruit, one for every man on board was unloaded, a welcome present from President Roosevelt. Meetings between Churchill and Roosevelt went on and the ships' boats went to and fro. We saw more and more of the Americans. As we got to know them better, I learned that we knew more about America than they knew about Britain, even if much of our knowledge was based on American films. Their friendliness and desire to reach an early familiarity lacked a certain sincerity. I realised too that we were reaching the wrong conclusion in assuming that they were from similar backgrounds, interests and understanding to our own just because they spoke English. A common language made for easy communication but I sensed a strong Germanic trait in their approach, usually with purpose and efficiency and not caring overly much for subtlety. I later came to value friendships with individual Americans but only after each of us had recognised the considerable gap that existed between us.

SS Augusta sailed on Tuesday, 12th of August and, soon afterwards, the Prince of Wales weighed anchor and proceeded with an additional escort of two American destroyers. As the Americans were not familiar with the British signalling system, all signals were passed in plain language by lamp. We were somewhat intrigued at the possible consequence of an encounter with enemy forces. Fortunately this was not put to the test although, at one stage, we were obliged to alter course to avoid the presence of U boats.

On Friday the 15th, an hour before dusk, we altered course to overtake a convoy of some seventy ships and sailed through the middle of the convoy of merchantmen. Their speed was about eight knots. Ours was 22. As we passed them at a relative speed of fourteen, we flew a signal in international code – Good luck – Churchill. The response from three grimy, grey, well-laden merchant ships was immediate. They sounded their fog horns and sirens and soon every ship was flying flag V in response to Churchill who stood on the flying bridge with upraised arm showing his famous victory sign. Churchill thrived on this affectionate demonstration and, on drawing ahead, the Prince of Wales was ordered to make a turn and pass down the flank of the convoy until we were well astern. At this point we steamed through the columns of ships to a resounding reception by the crews of the merchantmen. It was an impressive display of loyalty and affection, a memorable one for all of us. The sight of those merchant ships plodding towards Britain in long grey columns in the evening sunshine made a deep impression on me. There was none of the glamour for them, nor the means to defend themselves in case of attack and if attack did come, it would be by stealth and without warning.

The Prince of Wales continued at 22 knots and the weather improved although it was cold for the time of year. The perpetual light of mid-summer was giving way to a period of darkness of a few hours during the early hours of the morning but, on the morning of August 16th, close to Iceland, the moon was full and its light flooded the sea for miles around us. As we zig-zagged through the night and I came off watch, rather than turn in before being called out again to dawn action stations (a routine precautionary measure at sea during the war) I remained on deck watching our foaming wake. Looking for'ard at the massive superstructure I began to feel, for the first time, that I now belonged to this great ship even if my contribution was insignificant.

One's duties were limited as a midshipman of the watch. They were mostly of a menial nature designed to gradually initiate one into the working of the ship. All telephones to the bridge were his responsibility and he soon learned to locate each one by its separate call sound in the dark. He kept the log, changed the special discs to the visual challenge lamp to a pre-set code every four hours, calculated each leg of the zig-zag and called time to alter course and assisted the officer of the watch in keeping station when in company. During the quiet hours of the middle watch, a congenial officer of the watch might allow the midshipman to take over the conning of the ship but, more often than not, he was occupied with the making of the cocoa. This ritual was performed behind the bridge with the messengers who, having brought up a can (known as a fanny) of steaming water from below, he would join in scraping slivers from large solid blocks of naval issue pure cocoa to which, when dissolved, was added tinned milk and sugar. A midshipman's skill in supervising this brew ensured the confidence of his officers but it was in the performance of one of his other duties, shaking the officers of the relieving watch during the night, which required considerable diplomatic skill and a good memory for every officer's idiosyncracy as to how he should be awakened. Some required one to merely open the door, call out the time and tell them the weather, some wanted the light switched on and one officer would not wake up until his nose had been held. Another instructed the midshipmen not to leave the cabin until he was upright and his eyes open while another required a second call on one's way back to the bridge. I was told that it was only proper for an officer to fulfil this duty as it was forbidden for a sailor to lay his hands on a sleeping officer. I wondered how they managed on smaller ships, light cruisers and destroyers because they did not carry midshipmen.

The Prince of Wales entered Hvalfjord on the morning of August the 16th and moored close astern to Ramilles. It was two and a half months since our last visit. The weather was decidedly warmer with no snow on the surrounding hills. Mr Churchill and a vast retinue of staff officers disembarked for a journey to Reykjavik where he took the opportunity of visiting the American garrison which had been stationed in Iceland for some time.

Close on midnight, the Prince of Wales weighed anchor and proceeded with a screen of three escorting destroyers. We entered Scapa Flow early in the morning of August 18th and secured our usual berth where Mr Churchill, together with the first sea lord and other personages, disembarked with their respective staffs. On the previous evening, Mr Churchill had visited the gunroom as our guest, a momentous occasion for us all.

We were all conscious that we had taken a part in an historic occasion but, at the time, we were more interested in the mail as it was brought aboard. As was customary on the first night back in harbour, a raucous party developed after dinner when some midshipmen from the Rodney came on board and the opportunity was taken to debag and dubbin me as an initiation to show that, as a new boy, I was getting a bit above myself. Jim Errington also had this treatment for failing to show proper respect. Perhaps because of this a bond was formed between us and we became firm friends.

HMS Prince of Wales returns to Scapa Flow after Atlantic Charter Meeting 18th Aug 1941. Ships company mans the side to bid farewell to Mr Churchill and party.

Jim Errington was the son of a well to do business man in the City. The family had no connections with the navy and, after Dartmouth, Jim had tried to transfer to the Indian navy. A number of cadets had been appointed to the R.I.N. When Jim heard that I had spent my first few years in India and that my parents, whom I had not seen since before the war, were still there, his curiosity of all things Indian was insatiable. He would bombard me with questions but I could only tell him of my childhood memories. These were somewhat clouded by time but seemed to fit his romantic ideas of that country, an India of which Kipling wrote, burning plains, cool hill stations and faithful Gunga Dins. I could not disabuse him because I had even less of an idea of India at that time than he did. I was able to convey to him that unique smell blended from the odours of dust, wood smoke, cow-dung, humanity and rotting vegetation mingled with the scent of marigold and jasmine which had always meant home to me.

Britain's fortunes in the Mediterranean were at their lowest ebb during the latter part of 1941 and she was facing a desperate situation. Greece and Crete had fallen to the Germans in the spring which enabled them to fly aircraft over the whole of the central and eastern Mediterranean thus confining Admiral Cunningham's fleet to the south eastern regions. The Axis armies were also in full control of the North African shoreline. Only Malta remained in our hands as a base from which the Axis supply lines to North Africa could be attacked but, as the year progressed, this too looked somewhat tenuous as fuel, food and ammunition fell to dangerous levels. Convoys of supplies were having to fight through under heavy escort from Gibraltar and losses of ships and men mounted with each attempt.

The relative calm of Scapa Flow seemed a long way away from these events and, although we were aware of the debacle that had befallen us in the eastern Mediterranean in the spring, we were kept unaware of the true nature of Britain's strategic situation at that time. In July, the Nelson with the cruisers Edinburgh, Manchester and Arethusa had been detached from the Home Fleet to the Mediterranean. When the Prince of Wales returned to Scapa Flow after repairs had been completed, the anchorage was somewhat depleted of ships. In late August, the Rodney also left and, following a series of exercises, the Prince of Wales prepared for sea. On September 17th, the Prince of Wales weighed anchor and proceeded at 14.00 hours. The voyage to Gibraltar was without incident. We passed a medium sized convoy off Cape Trafalgar which was obviously heading for the Mediterranean. For myself, it was a painful time because I was severely reprimanded for a foolish lapse.

It was my duty to shake the officers of the relieving middle watch on the second night out. I left the bridge at twenty past eleven and did my rounds of the various cabins and then I went in search of Jim Errington who was my relief. He was not in his hammock but I found him sleeping in one of the green rexine-covered chairs in the corner of the gunroom which was a serious breach of gunroom rules. I woke him but it was only twenty to twelve and he was already fully dressed and had his coat over his knees. He told me to sit down and give him a few minutes to come round and I did so which was a foolish thing to do because I was dog tired and had been troubled with a succession of sleepless nights with a grumbling tooth which no amount of aspirin seemed to allay. Within minutes I, too, started to doze and was suddenly jerked awake by Jim who was shouting at me and indicating the gunroom clock which stood at five minutes past midnight. We both dashed for the bridge and reached it in record time but, by then, the watch had been relieved and the captain himself was on the bridge. This was an awkward moment for Jim Errington had broken the rules by sleeping in the gunroom and I had gone to sleep while technically still on watch. The officer of the watch was furious and, without interrogating us, merely snapped that we were to report to the Snotty Nurse in the morning. Needless to say, I was full of apprehension for the rest of the night and could not sleep. I dozed until the call for dawn action stations was sounded.

The next morning, we were both escorted to the Snotty Nurse by the gunroom lieutenant. When we told him what had happened, he blazed at us, reminded us that had we been sailors, we would have been punished by a spell in the cells or, as boy seamen, caned. But we did not tell him the whole truth. We had agreed that I should take the blame on the principle of being hung as a sheep as for a lamb. I therefore told the Snotty Nurse that I had a few minutes to spare before shaking Errington and I had gone to the gunroom for a cigarette and, inadvertently, dropped off to sleep and it was midnight before I came round. He was not entirely taken in because he expressed surprise that I smoked, a habit I had only just started. Nevertheless, he dismissed Errington and proceeded to give me what is known in the navy as 'a bottle'. I was finally dismissed and, because of my relative inexperience and my good record so far, I was let off by being confined to the ship for a month. We had no idea how long we would be at sea but the buzz round the ship was that we were going to the Mediterranean and the thought of being confined to ship in places such as Gibraltar and Malta was somewhat galling. I was not to know how dangerous the Mediterranean was and that one could only go to Malta if one fought one's way there and, most certainly, a passage to the eastern Mediterranean was out of the question.

When we arrived in Gibraltar on Saturday, September 21st, we found a much larger concentration of ships than we had ever seen in Scapa Flow. Both the Nelson and the Rodney were there, massive, high out of the water with that peculiar fore-shortened stern which, I gather, was a design afterthought. The famous Ark Royal was there too and the cruisers, Edinburgh, Manchester, Arethusa and Kenya and a large number of destroyers. Clearly an operation of some magnitude was in the offing.

The air was balmy and our eyes delighted in a change of scenery from the bleakness of Scapa Flow where the days were rapidly drawing in and the islands beginning to take a wintry aspect. We refuelled, took on ammunition and stores and many of the gunroom officers went ashore. I was, of course, still on board. I equipped myself with a pair of ship's glasses, found my way to a vantage point on the after structure and closely scrutinised the shore.

Gibraltar is topographically splendid, a thin finger of granite overlooking a wide sweep of a bay some five miles across to Algeciras in Spain where, no doubt the Germans or Spaniards in their pay watched us. War seemed far away as I looked across the bay, crammed with ships of every description on that beautiful, mellow afternoon. It was from news gained from our old friends on the Rodney that it was, in fact, very close. It was not long before we found out for ourselves. On Wednesday, September 24th, we were signalled up with the pipe, 'Close all scuttles,' followed by 'Special sea duty men' and later by 'Hands fall in for leaving harbour.'

We proceeded in company with the Nelson (flying the flag of Admiral Sir James Somerville), Rodney and Ark Royal. The cruiser squadron was under the command of Rear Admiral Burroughs, flying his flag in Kenya. The convoy was composed of nine ships and it was intended that the main covering force of battleships and the Ark Royal would accompany us as far as the Narrows (between Cape

36

Bon and Sicily) while the cruiser squadron would continue escorting the convoy over the final section to Malta.

This was the first time that the Prince of Wales had taken part in convoy duties and we found the slow speed of twelve knots to be in strong contrast to our normal speed of twenty knots or more. The first day was uneventful but we all knew that convoys to Malta were being fiercely contested by the enemy and tension remained high. Once again, preliminary work on preparing the ship for action was started and was carried out throughout the day. For those of us in the air defence position, it looked as though our main adversaries were to be enemy shore-based aircraft while the heavy screen of eighteen destroyers would deal with U-boat attacks. After months in northern waters, the return to more normal hours of light and darkness and the almost perfect sunny weather did much to raise our morale. It soon became clear, however, that the Prince of Wales had not been designed to operate in the tropics as her ventilation system was unable to cope with the heat which rapidly built up below decks, despite the fact that summer had already passed and the weather on deck was almost ideal. The midshipmen's sleeping space was particularly hot but we were forbidden to sleep on deck as the ship was closed up to defence stations.

On the second day out from Malta, the skies and sea remained clear while the ship was exercised at close range weapon firing whereby the pom-poms and oerlikons were fired at successive single air bursts from a 5.25 inch gun. Later that day, a number of submarine contacts were obtained by the destroyers and depth charges were dropped but without result. The Ark Royal flew off her aircraft at various times as air cover force but no interceptions were made and the radar screen remained uninterrupted. That evening, the captain addressed the ship's company over the ship's address system and told us that while we had enjoyed a quiet voyage so far, this could not be expected to prevail on the next day and attacks by aircraft and, possibly, Italian surface ships could be expected at any time from dawn onwards.

The next day, we closed up to action stations before dawn, a routine performed every day whilst at sea but on this occasion, a heightened sense of anticipation prevailed. We did not have long to wait. As the sky began to lighten and transform itself into another bright Mediterranean day, radar echoes of unidentified aircraft were picked up some 90 miles to the north east flying out of Sardinia. We turned into the wind to allow the Ark Royal to fly off aircraft and, at the same time, there was intense activity on the air defence position as radar reports were received and all communications with the directors and secondary armament re-checked. From the radar plots, it was becoming clear that a major air attack was developing and soon afterwards we heard that the Ark Royal's aircraft had intercepted a large group of torpedo bombers. Almost immediately after this, groups of aircraft were sighted low on the horizon where they began to split up into attacking groups. Our port secondary director above our heads began to track and soon we reacted to the sound of our twin 5.25s engaging with rapid concerted salvoes with their distinctive whiplash crack filling the air which was almost as ear shattering as the blast from the larger 14-inch guns. Immediately the horizon was filled with black bursting shells as the Nelson and the guns of the cruisers joined in the barrage. As the range closed, I watched incredulously as the aircraft flew on, seemingly oblivious of our concentrated fire bursting above and below them where the sea was now a boiling cauldron as thousands of shrapnel fragments struck the water. I saw one aircraft begin to flame and soon afterwards crash into the sea. Immediately afterwards, the two sets of pom-poms immediately below the bridge began firing with their characteristic 'whump whump' sound. They soon ceased firing however as faults began to develop, much to the chagrin of the Air Defence Officer who kept asking the officer of quarters for an explanation. Then came the order, 'Check, check, check.' The guns fell silent and suddenly, there were no aircraft to be seen.

The attack had lasted about ten minutes and I began to realise that even for those of us in exposed positions, it was difficult to keep track of what was happening, conscious only of the rapid fire of our 5.25s and the close range weapons. Confirming this impression, we heard from the bridge, that the Nelson had been hit by an aerial torpedo which none of us had seen or heard. From our vantage point, we could now see the Nelson drawing out of her station but she seemed unaffected by the damage. In my ignorance, I asked one of the lieutenants if she would sink but he explained that an aerial torpedo was generally much smaller, about 18 inches, than the 21 inch torpedoes carried by destroyers or submarines and a battleship would have to be hit many times with these smaller torpedoes to be sunk. I had good cause to remember those words later on although I was naturally forced to refrain from reminding him of them.

This short initial action was followed by a lull of some hours during which time we remained at action stations. Breakfast was brought to everyone – hot steaming cups of tea and a galvanised container filled with 'tiddley oggies'. There was much hilarity and joking about the war being stopped for breakfast until someone reminded us that Italians never ate breakfast and would be back fairly soon. Within half an hour there were radar reports of large groups (20 plus) of unidentified aircraft or bogeys closing on the convoy from a slightly different direction. (All aircraft echoes were classed as unidentified until confirmed as either friendly or bandits). Once again the Royal Ark's fighters flew to intercept and soon there were black specks on the horizon flying towards us at speed. This time the cruisers opened fire with their main armaments in the form of an air burst barrage and soon afterwards our 5.25s were engaged. I was glued to a head-set passing orders to the port pom-poms which had cleared their problems with jammed ammunition. I happened to look up and saw a flaming aircraft falling into the sea and another crashing astern of it. There were muffled cheers from everyone but we were very soon sobered by the news that the second aircraft was one of Ark Royal's who had followed the Italian torpedo plane too enthusiastically to be met by the equally enthusiastic fire from the Prince of Wales. We were all cast down by this mistake and it was clear that some form of drill was necessary to prevent our own aircraft from becoming embroiled once the enemy began its final run in.

A further air attack developed later in the day but seemed to lack the determination of the earlier ones and was soon beaten off by Ark Royal's fighters. While this attack was being beaten off, we were electrified to hear that the Italian fleet had been sighted from the air and was approaching the convoy.

At 14.30 hours, we formed up with Rodney, Edinburgh, Manchester and Arethusa under the command of Rear Admiral Curties and increased speed to 27 knots gradually working up to full speed as we headed north eastwards towards the enemy battle squadron. After idling along at the staid speed of 12 - 15 knots, except when taking avoiding action, the Prince of Wales now vibrated with increased engine revolutions, the exhaust fans of the fore funnel almost deafening us with their increased roar as she thrust her way through very calm seas. Both the Edinburgh and Manchester threw up high wakes with their raked funnels giving an impression of high speed aggression. It was an awe inspiring sight and one of the more memorable ones. Memories of actions are always confused in the minds of those taking part but the sights that remain with me are the most stirring or placid ones – the Prince of Wales zig-zagging through a calm sea in a bright, cold, clear moonlight: destroyers slipping through Switha at Scapa in the late evening light or, as in this case, cruisers under full speed, ensigns full out and dipping and rising in the clear Mediterranean swell.

Torpedo bombers had been launched from the Ark Royal but, after a few hours, we heard that they had failed to locate the Italians who had presumably returned home. The squadron immediately reduced speed and turned away southwards to rejoin the damaged Nelson and the convoy. When we rejoined the convoy, it had reached the Narrows at which point, the convoy went on ahead to Malta with an escort of cruisers while Kenya, Prince of Wales and Nelson with screening destroyers turned to the westward and made course for Gibraltar where we arrived without incident on 1st October.

After refuelling at Gibraltar, the Prince of Wales returned to Scapa Flow and by the 5th of October, we were back in the main anchorage at our usual berth. There was an unmistakable improvement in morale on this return journey. We all felt we had acquitted ourselves well by shooting down two enemy aircraft although somewhat chastened by shooting down one of our own in the process. But there were signs that the ship was functioning much more smoothly, breakdowns were less frequent and men moved about the ship with an accustomed air. We were also conscious that we had been worked hard within the first few months of being commissioned and had seen far more sea-time and action than our sister ship, the flagship King George V.

Monday, 20th of October was the start of another week and we settled down to the ennui of Scapa Flow in normal harbour routine. I was still confined to the ship and, therefore, unable to visit other ships nor accompany other midshipmen who went ashore for long walks only to end up eating hard boiled eggs and drinking whisky in a local pub. By afternoon, there were imperceptible signs that we were about to put to sea again, becoming clearer in the evening when ammunition lighters and the water tanker came alongside. Ammunitioning and storing went on throughout with a sense of urgency which stimulated a spate of rumours.

The two most persistent rumours were the contrasting ones of either Northern Russia or the Far East, the latter being the favourite. There were many who held that the British would hardly tie up one of its new battleships in the peaceful Far East when it was essential she kept as many battleships as possible in the Home Fleet. On the other hand, the situation in the Far East was beginning to look ominous since the summer of 1941. Even though the two protagonists were America and Japan, it was certain that Britain would automatically be involved should hostilities break out there.

Feelings in the gunroom were divided. There were some who were sure that we would remain with the Home Fleet while others who surreptitiously began buying up sports equipment from other midshipmen in the fleet looking forward to a bit of peacetime navy, tropical nights, alluring Eastern ladies and exotic food. I belonged to the second school. I was beginning to loathe Scapa Flow and I had always had a strong compulsion to travel to strange places. Unlike the others, I thought there might be a slender chance that I could see my family again. I would have, however, preferred to stay in the Mediterranean where the climate was equable, the bases were foreign and exciting and there was plenty of action. This desire for remaining in active theatres was not, however founded on youthful bravado but was a commonly expressed desire by many as a reaction against long days spent moored in Scapa Flow or endless days and nights on patrol searching empty, iron-hard and bleak horizons with monotonous regularity. Under these circumstances, a change in routine, even the appearance of the enemy was welcome. Such was the confidence of the Royal Navy that it never occurred to us that we might get the worst of any such encounter. When we sailed two days later, it was with some relief that I looked upon the bleak, sombre islands of Scapa Flow for the last time.

The Prince of Wales proceeded through the Hoxa Gate at 06.00 hours on Thursday, 23rd of October where we were joined by the destroyers Electra and Express as escorts. We proceeded through the Minches southward to Greenock on the Clyde where we arrived at 09.00 hours the next day and anchored in the river. Within an hour lighters were alongside with additional fuel. Stores were taken on board. A number of new seamen drafts joined the ship and, later in the day, a party of R.A.F. men with a conducting officer arrived on board whom, we soon learned, were on their way to Africa. Our destination now seemed certain to be the Far East via the Cape. This was confirmed later when I went to the lower chartroom to find the Navigating Officer checking our supply of charts and particularly those for a route to the east via the Cape. I was also told of a change of arrangements as we expected an admiral and a large staff to join at any time.

Early the next morning a party of six RNVR sub-lieutenants joined the ship and a number came to live with us in the gunroom. These men were additional cipher officers and we all began to feel that we were about to embark on a voyage of some importance. The cipher officers sent to live with us were a close-mouthed trio and nothing definite of our destination was gleaned from them, as befitted their training. Perhaps, like us, they too knew very little.

During the afternoon of Saturday, October 25th, Acting Admiral, Sir Tom Phillips, KCB, accompanied by his Chief of staff, Rear Admiral A.R.E. Palliser DSC, a supporting team of specialist officers and flag lieutenants, hoisted his flag on the Prince of Wales and, within a few hours, 'special sea duty men' was being piped preparatory to leaving our mooring.

The Admiral was a physically unimpressive man of unusually small stature and a cold, pale face. He had a reputation of being something of a martinet and was known to one and all as Tom Thumb or Tich. His chief of Staff, Rear Admiral Palliser was a taller man with an unsmiling, tight lipped, intimidating manner and was said to be a strict disciplinarian as befitted a gunnery specialist and former Captain of Whale Island – H.M.S. Excellent. Another officer in the Admiral's staff who was very gunnery was Commander Michael Goodenough, DSO., the staff officer and nephew of the famous Admiral 'Barge' Goodenough of the Harwich Force during the First World War. He was a heavily built man with iron grey hair and a florid complexion. We were all warned to steer clear of the gunnery element of the Admiral's staff whom it was said, 'ate midshipmen for tea'. It must be admitted that the only time I had a message to deliver to Rear Admiral Palliser, he offered me a kindly word, quite out of keeping with his austere demeanour.

At one p.m. the Prince of Wales weighed anchor and proceeded down the Clyde where we made an impressive and powerful sight with an Admiral's flag and a white ensign at the main, our pennants at the yardarm, straight lines of seamen on the upper deck and the marine band thumping out a sprightly air on the quarter deck. And as the strains of music floated over the glittering waters of the Clyde, back came the thin reedy notes of bosuns' pipes from other vessels saluting us.

After clearing the 'tail of the bank' and the Clyde boom, Errington and I walked for a while on the quarter deck and watched the coast of Britain slowly recede in the clear, pale sun of a late autumn afternoon bathing the low, green hills in a silent watery light. We stood watching for a long time, both thinking our private thoughts, knowing we were probably heading for the other side of the world, clinging to the familiar and reluctant to surrender it to the distance.

In the years that followed, I often forced myself to think of that moment and it is now deeply etched in my mind. Now there was

43

work to be done, duties to attend to and we both went our separate ways. First nights at sea were always strange, the accustomed calm now disturbed by the heavy vibration, ventilation fans at a higher pitch and scuttles and deadlights firmly closed and which would remain so until we entered harbour again.

We headed west-nor-west all through the first night to the north of Ireland and well out into the Atlantic before altering course southward on the second day. Our destroyer escort of two had been increased by the addition of Hesperus and, on the third day, Legion joined company to release Express and Electra who were detached to Horta in the Azores for refuelling. They both returned the next day and Legion and Hesperus parted company and made for Gibraltar.

As the Prince of Wales and her two escorting destroyers sailed southwards through a moderate westerly swell at a steady 18-20 knots, the weather became warmer with each passing day and the ship's company settled down into a routine of cruising watches. One quarter of the ship's armament was shut up and everyone kept a four hour watch with eight hours off. However, the splitting of the dog watches between 4 and 8 p.m. into two periods of two hours each was a device whereby everyone kept a different watch every day and night. On the fourth night, we were able to sleep through which we called our 'night-in'. All hands were engaged on other tasks during the day which commenced with precautionary action stations at first light, followed by cleaning ship, breakfast, gun drill for some and numerous important maintenance tasks. In the boiler and engine rooms, stokers and artificers kept up a steady round of watch keeping, responding with slight, delicate adjustment to changes in revolutions ordered from the bridge, overhauling and maintaining the vast and complicated power system.

On the eighth day out of the Clyde, we entered the tropics with a change in wind direction to the north-east and a following sea. With the wind on the quarter, sulphur laden fumes were drawn into the ventilation system and, with the increasing heat, life below deck became a trial. We had all changed into white, tropical rig – white cap covers, white open-necked shirts and short trousers and tended to spend as much time as possible on deck. Sleep below decks was difficult and, at night, we removed the mattress and blanket from our hammocks and rigged up camp beds, took them to the quarter deck and laid them on the open deck under the stars. We usually tried to find a berth beneath the overhang of the main after 14 inch gun turret to shelter from the shower of soot usually blown from the funnels during the middle watch which, if the wind was light and for'ard, often fell in black blobs on the quarter deck. As we progressed well into the tropics and entered what meteorologists call 'the inter-tropical convergence zone' or 'monsoon front', we were also often drenched by sudden rain squalls during the night. Most officers kept to their cabins, lying stripped under the punkah louvre, quite a few of the midshipmen endeavoured to sleep on deck as did many of the crew. Although not forbidden, it was a practice that was not encouraged, if not actually frowned upon, with a frequently blackened face or sodden blanket as a more positive deterrent. Adding to our discomfort was the outbreak of prickly heat which covered our bodies in red nettle-like rash and itched maddeningly. As an added complication, many developed what was called 'dhobi itch' in the crotch and under the arm-pits which aggravated the discomforts of the prickly heat on the rest of the body. Many treatments were used to treat the problem but none were even slightly effective. The only cure was exposure to a cold blast of air for which we would have to wait.

We entered Freetown to refuel on the 5th of November, the capital of Sierra Leone. Freetown with its dark green jungle-clad slopes leading to the mountain vaguely resembled the outline of a crouching lion, from which it took its Spanish name. It looked the veritable white man's grave. Despite a large wartime influx of naval and air force personnel, an enervating miasma of tropical torpor seemed to lie over the town and harbour. Freetown, I found, took its name from an experiment in humanitarian imperialism. Created as a British colony specifically for the resettlement of freed slaves as a necessary adjunct to the abolition of the slave trade, early in the nineteenth century, a large number of freed slaves, together with a number of deported English prostitutes, were sent to Freetown and over the years, a distinct culture evolved – British, Christian,

45

Evangelical and of mixed European and African descent. We were given shore leave that afternoon and we were anxious to get off the ship after six weeks on board (my punishment having expired on the day before we left Scapa Flow). I went ashore with Errington. I was glad I did for I found Freetown to be quite a remarkable little town which belied its tropical backwater appearance from the sea. Some streets were surprisingly elegant, faced with houses of yellow ochre-coloured sandstone, some with Georgian facades. The people seemed unaffected by a climate which remained constant and enervating throughout the year. I returned to the ship in the early evening feeling strangely refreshed by the sights and smells of wet earth and vegetation, a different people and the aroma of strange foods. But there was a feeling of mystery too – a strange mixture of voodoo and Christianity: imagined dark deeds at night and choir boys singing in their hybrid language in the Anglican Cathedral overlooking the elegant harbour steps.

We sailed the next day and, for the first two days out, we were escorted by successive flights of Sunderland flying boats which were based at Freetown until finally we reached the limit of their range and we were alone once more. When we reached the Equator, the traditional crossing the line ceremony was held and for a few hours the war was forgotten and the Prince of Wales resembled a peace time passenger liner as strangely bedecked figures cavorted on deck. With that, the ship reverted to a steady routine as we rounded the bulge of Africa and set a course for the Cape of Good Hope. Frequent rain squalls drenched the ship and our precautionary, continuous zig-zag course, maintained throughout the day and night, had the added effect of sometimes enabling us to dodge these squalls but, on other occasions, sailing directly into them. It added interest to long, boring watches.

It was during forenoon of one of these days that a marine was brought before the officer of the watch on the bridge under the escort of two men who appeared to be holding him up. He had been found drunk and looked it with his eyes clouded over and his face a ghastly colour. He was soon marched off after being given a 'Commander's report.' I later heard the details of this somewhat extraordinary happening. In the dry goods store, such oddments as boat's compasses, odd bits of tackle and large tins of food were normally stored and an able seaman appointed as its guardian. This particularly enterprising seaman had discovered that by draining the alcohol from the compasses and diluting it with the juice from tinned prunes, a devastating concoction was produced. He named it prunella and sold it at about three-pence a tot to the many marines and sailors who beat a hasty path to the dry goods store, successfully avoiding the Regulating Petty Officers. It was only when the marine was discovered drunk that the whole operation was brought to light, somewhat to the embarrassment of the Master-at-Arms.

As the Prince of Wales sailed south eastwards on a converging course with the coast of Africa, we entered the happy hunting ground of U-boats and, earlier in the war, of German surface raiders too, such as the Graf Spee. Extra vigilance was ordered. The two destroyers acted as a screen and kept us on a continual asdic watch which threw a sweeping series of 'pings' or sound impulses ahead. When one of these sound impulses hit a solid object within about half a mile, an echo would travel back to the asdic receiver and, from the elapsed time and direction of the asdic dome, a distance and bearing of the underwater object was instantly made known. This underwater listening and echo probing device sometimes picked up schools of fish or whales or the noises of other ships' screws but a good operator could usually distinguish the echo by very small differences in character; a submarine always gave an unmistakeable bell like sound echoing from its steel hull. We sailed on however without incident and, after crossing the Tropic of Capricorn and into the stronger, colder Benguella current, which has its origins in the Antarctic, the air noticeably cooled; our prickly heat rashes disappeared almost overnight and we changed out of tropical kit.

There was also a marked change in the weather as the wind began to strengthen from the south-west and, for the first time, we saw a number of albatross. With a wing span of over ten feet, pure white wings with black tips, the wandering Albatross is the world's largest bird and inhabits the southern oceans of the globe. Closely observing one of these birds, I was struck by its regular and precise

47

flight pattern. After following the wake of the ship, gliding above the stern, it would suddenly sheer off abeam at an angle of forty-five degrees until it was but a speck on the horizon, where it would turn ninety degrees and glide back towards the ship on a perfect intercepting course to remain with us for another stretch without so much as a flicker of its immense wings - a beautiful bird, the perfection of effortless motion and wonderful to watch. Somehow one could not agree with Coleridge that this bird was the symbol of man's guilt.

On the 11th of November, which happened to be my 18th birthday, I was on deck watching the giant, wandering albatross gliding in an oscillating motion just astern of us when I saw a smaller bird flying alongside on a steady southward course. We soon overhauled it and I instantly recognised it as an Arctic tern, completely white except for the black hangman's hood over its head and eyes and a red beak, flying with a steady wing beat and a characteristic tilt of the head. At first I thought that maybe I was mistaken but then I remembered, this was November and that these birds usually migrate from the Arctic to the Antarctic and back again in alternate summers. Some years later, I learned that their route from the Arctic, covering some 8,000 miles, takes them on a great circle to Labrador then across the Atlantic to the west coast of Africa, thence southwards along the African coast to the Cape and on southwards towards Antarctica where they spend the northern winter. Soon this little bird dropped astern as I watched fascinated. For some absurd reason, perhaps because it was my birthday, I took it as a good omen and pondered on the strength, the stamina and above all the superior navigational instinct of this small, graceful bird.

On the next day, the wind began to increase and visibility was much reduced by clouds and rain and I noticed there were many more albatross and large brown storm petrels around which often presaged the onset of a storm. And so it was to be, for the weather began to deteriorate with winds above 20 knots, driving rain and huge waves. The destroyers were soon in trouble and were forced to reduce speed as the heavy seas threatened to overcome them at a speed of 18 knots. The Prince of Wales, however, ploughed on leaving the Electra and Express astern to make the best speed they could and head for the naval base at Simonstown whilst we headed towards Cape Town.

At first light on the morning of Sunday, November 16th, we reduced speed and sailed southward into Table Bay. The weather was overcast and cloudy but calmer. It was some time before we were able to distinguish the massive ramparts of the extraordinary tubular massif of Table Mountain., the two lesser conical peaks on either side and the city of Cape Town draped over its lower slopes. From the shore came the smells of land, some familiar but others more exotic and one that I recognised immediately from my Indian childhood, the smell of rain on warm earth. We entered the dock basin and secured alongside after being fussily manoeuvred by two tugs manned by Europeans, Africans and men of mixed race who all stared curiously at us. The Royal Navy's base on the South Atlantic station was at Simonstown on False Bay and it was, I discovered later, comparatively rare for warships to dock at Cape Town. However it was clear that we wished to advertise our presence in these water thus confirming news reports we had heard during the voyage whereby it had been announced that 'a powerful naval force had been sent to the Far East.' We all wondered where the rest of the ships were.

Cape Town held out the promise of a welcome change from wartime England to all of those aboard but we were quite unprepared for the extraordinary hospitality displayed by the hundreds of South Africans who converged at the dock gates in their cars to carry seamen and marines off to their homes, farms and on sight seeing trips. Errington and I decided to go ashore in the afternoon although we had been warned that everything would be closed. Undeterred, we set off to walk to the city, the main street of which ran from the docks directly through the centre of town. We had not gone far when a car with a family, including two very pretty girls, crawled past and subjected us to a close scrutiny. Having decided that we looked presentable or perhaps innocent and harmless enough, the car stopped. A well dressed man emerged, introduced himself as John Seago and asked us if they could show us Cape Town. We accepted with alacrity and were soon being driven through the centre of town and were shown places of interest and various landmarks. We were much more interested in the family and particularly the two girls, one was their daughter and the other was her friend.

Mr Seago had been born in Cornwall. He was a marine engineer and held a senior position with a large local ship repair firm. He had been in South Africa for twenty years. He had not lost his English accent and was eager to show off his adopted country. It wasn't long before we learned of his contempt for the other half of South Africa's white population, the Afrikaners, many of whom opposed South Africa's entry into the war against Germany. He ignored the many blacks and people of mixed race or, at least, he hardly mentioned their presence. Although we are now acutely aware of racial problems facing South Africa, these hardly impinged on our consciousness at that time and while Mr Seago attempted to analyse the local political situation for us with frequent interruptions to point out some local landmark. Both Errington and I were trying to engage the attention of the two girls in the back seat. Mrs Seago, I thought, was beginning to regret their offer to drive us round and, after a while, she must have decided that the intimacy of four young bodies squeezed into the back seat was beginning to produce an undesirable effect on her young charges, for she suggested we stop and take a walk now that we had left the town behind. Soon we were walking through Mediterranean type umbrella pine woods high up in a pass between Table Mountain and Devils Peak with glorious views to the north and east and Cape Town at our feet. Although it was early summer, the air was like wine and crystal clear and we could see for miles. Later we were taken to their home, a long drive through leafy, beautifully kept suburbs to Rondebosch, a few miles south of Cape Town itself.

As it was warm, we sat out on the lawn in the twilight, drinking beer and generally being as agreeable as we could with Mr Seago and some neighbours who had casually dropped in. We were both taken with the informal friendliness of these people to be completely overcome by more beer, the relaxed atmosphere, a magnificent meal (the likes of which neither of us had seen for a long time) and the

50

presence of two vivacious girls. We were driven back through dimmed-out streets and allowed brief embraces in the back seat, parting at the dock gates with promises to see each other the next day. After careful instructions and telephone numbers were exchanged, we returned on board in an euphoria of pleasurable feelings to find other members of the gunroom exchanging similar experiences in a relaxed, happy mood. There were one or two who had been obliged to stay on board and were now forced to listen to our accounts with unconcealed envy.

We had expected to stay in Cape Town for at least a week so I was not overly concerned when I was told to stay on board for watch keeping duties the next day. Errington went ashore and returned late the next evening looking like the proverbial cat. Early next morning, we heard that we would be sailing shortly in response to urgent orders. I therefore had to be content with writing a quick letter to the one girl, the friend of the family, and another to the family themselves thanking them for their hospitality with a promise to write. I did so from Singapore but I never heard or saw them again.

Thursday, November 18th, the Prince of Wales cast off at 16.00 hours and was manoeuvred out of the dock basin by tugs into Table Bay. We turned south for Cape Point and our rendezvous with the Electra and Express. Once clear of the southern tip of Africa, we steadied on a north-easterly course to pass south of the island of Mauritius. We were all in a chastened mood as we left Cape Town, many of us having made instant and spontaneous attachments and been given a very brief taste of a style of life which had almost disappeared from wartime England.

On the afternoon of 23rd of November, the Prince of Wales put in briefly to Grand Port, Mauritius to refuel. We sailed shortly afterwards. Mauritius seemed remote, detached from the war as indeed it was. It was better known only as the home of the dodo, now long extinct. A brief view showed mountains rising dark and green to the north shrouded by thunder clouds at this time of the year. From Mauritius, (Darwin's elegantly constructed island) we proceeded northwards and back into the tropics with a return to tropical rig, shoals of flying fish disturbed by our bow wave, a stifling gunroom and hammock flat, prickly heat and nights spent on deck sometimes showered with soot and sometimes rain. Our one delight on this passage was fresh fruit which had been taken on board at Cape Town by our mess men. Grapes were out of season but there were oranges, lemons and pineapples and some enterprising spirits even managed to bring some Cape wine on board.

On the morning of the 26th November, we entered Addu Atoll through a narrow channel into a wide, palm fringed lagoon some miles across. Addu Atoll lies half a degree south of the Equator and at the southern end of the Maldive Island atoll chain which extends northwards for over five hundred miles. This long line of coral atolls hangs southwards like a pendant from the Indian sub-continent and presents a western barrier to the approaches of Ceylon. Remote and only sparsely populated, I was unaware of their existence until I noticed them on our charts. On Addu there was one small village on the southern end and the only British presence was a small party of soldiers who had been on the atoll for some months building gun emplacements. As a fleet anchorage it was ideal and the party of soldiers seemed to presage a move towards developing some such base here. Warm and idyllic, the atoll presented the tropical paradise one associated with the South Pacific but there were drawbacks. There was no water on the atoll and the small population were said to suffer from elephantiasis, a late complication of filaria transmitted by mosquito. After landing supplies and water to the party of soldiers, the Prince of Wales weighed and proceeded north.

We hove to off the narrow harbour entrance set in two long brownstone moles enclosing Colombo harbour late on November 27th. The coast line was flat but imposing terracotta and white buildings could be seen spread out to the south of the harbour as we slowly edged our way towards the narrow entrance. The long, elongated harbour was crowded with ships and among them the superstructure of an old P class battleship could be seen which turned out to be that of the Revenge whom we assumed would soon join us as part of the 'powerful naval force' we had heard so much about. We also knew that we would be joining company with the Repulse but there was no sign of her in the harbour.

Soon after we had moored, I was sent for by Commander Lawson, who showed me a signal pad containing two signals, the first from the naval headquarters shore asking if there was a Midshipman Percy aboard and the second an affirmative signal. I looked somewhat mystified and was unable to answer the Commander's interrogative look who then asked me if I had friends ashore. I could only say, 'No', but a few hours later another signal arrived saying that my father was in Colombo on detachment from the Indian Army and would be allowed to see me the following day. I was completely overcome by the news. Permission was granted for me to go ashore the next morning and meet him. However, he pre-empted me by arriving alongside in a boat at about nine o'clock the next day and was allowed to remain on the quarter deck while I was sent for and, shortly afterwards, allowed to go ashore.

The passenger jetty at the end of the harbour was almost a bazaar in itself where small caddies of Orange Pekoe tea were sold amongst other curio and bric-a-brac but, as we stopped on the concourse, it was, for me, India again – the ubiquitous rickshaws, battered old canvas-hooded taxis, the long colonnaded streets stretching away in all directions, the pungent smell of fish and betel nuts, humanity and the ever present cawing of kites. We were met by an army driver, shown to a car and were soon edging our way through the streets upwards, past the botanical gardens with its obligatory statue of Queen Victoria, and then southwards to the Galle Face Green, a vast expanse of immaculately kept lawn facing the sea. We passed the red brick pile of the Galle Face Hotel at the end of the Green and then along the road southwards for about twelve miles to Mount Lavinia where an ochre yellow hotel sat on a small promontory overlooking a long, straight, palm-backed, sandy beach receding into the distance in both directions. Once out of Colombo, the similarities with Northern India disappeared. Everything was a lush, overpowering green, dappled with the lighter green of the miles and miles of coconut plantations. This was the island of Serendip from which Horace Walpole had coined the word, serendipity in his play, The Three Princes of Serendip, the heroes of which were 'always making discoveries by accident and sagacity of things they were not in quest of.' As we drove along the coast road, I reflected on the equally happy accident of my father being in Ceylon. He went one better by describing our meeting as 'serendipitous'.

We arrived at the hotel just before lunch and sat out on the terrace where a breeze cooled the otherwise hot and humid air. I had not seen my father since 1937 when he and my mother had come to England but he did not seem to have grown any older. He was then fifty one years old and at an age when men seemed to stand still on a plateau before the gradual decline into old age. But now he was vital, his blue eyes twinkling from a deeply bronzed face dominated by his large Anglo-Irish nose and impeccably smart in his light coloured khaki uniform with his single row of Great War ribbons.

His career in the Far East had been unorthodox for he had originally come out in 1911 with a prominent London and Far Eastern commercial house operating in Burma. He spent his first term in Ragoon or travelling in upper Burma on various errands involving teak and rice. Somehow, I am not quite sure how, he managed to cut his first tour to three years and, in 1914, he was back in England. On the outbreak of war, he resigned and joined the Middlesex Regiment, the die-hards. He was later commissioned and sent to Egypt with his battalion where he took part in a little known campaign, the Senussi War in the latter part of 1915. While he was in Egypt, he added Arabic to Burmese as the second in a long list of eastern languages which he came to learn with accomplishment – Urdu, Hindi and Pushtu – and, perhaps because of his obvious talent for languages and a wide range in other scholarly interests, he was transferred to intelligence work. Later, in 1917, he was sent to Mesopotamia where he joined in the abortive campaign to relieve the Turkish siege of Kut. In that pestilential hell-hole, as he sometimes referred to Mesopotamia, he was successively ill with malaria and typhus and, having barely recovered, wounded in a skirmish at Aziziya near Baghdad and finally evacuated to India in 1917 after languishing for some time at Basra. He remained in India with a staff post doing very little for the remainder of the war but he soon decided that India held out an opportunity he was seeking and, towards the end of the war, applied for a commission in the Indian

Army. From all accounts, this proved to be a difficult, complicated and long drawn out procedure and only through the influence of influential friends did he succeed. He had, however, prepared his ground well as he had already passed the exam in Urdu and had assiduously begun a wide range of studies into aspects of Indian life and culture. He married my mother in 1922. She came from an army family, successive generations having served in India since before the time of the mutiny. I was born in Quetta in 1923 and my brother, Charles, eighteen months later in Simla.

My own recollection of India was one of continual moves from one cantonment to another only to be uprooted again every year for a retreat into the hills. The journeys always seemed to be a great undertaking proceeded by days of excited packing and a stream of orders issuing from my mother. But, above all, there was the fascination of the railway. Travel usually meant a long railway journey embarking from one teeming station which was a microcosm of India - the bustle, the yells of the vendors, the sweetmeat sellers, the water carriers, the hot tea men – tahsa char, garumi garum – and the beggars. The carriages we travelled in were quite grand. I was to compare them with English ones when I finally went to England but, to us, it was quite normal to have a large compartment with self-contained shower and lavatory, fans and ice compartment into which mysterious men would slip blocks of ice at various stops along the way which, with the aid of fans, would keep the space cool. We always carried our own bedding and something my mother never went without, boiled water. The journeys themselves were always stupendous, perhaps two days of continuous travel which seemed to stretch to eternity under an immense vaulted sky. Along the way was the ever changing kaleidoscope of a dun, rocky, spiky hard-baked land with sudden interjections of red from the gold mohur tree or the bright green of the irrigated valleys. At sundown, the air seemed to deflate and lose its fierce heat and the sky would turn to a dust laden red sometimes, in the colder months, streaked with horizontal layers of grey wispy smoke from evening dung fires hanging over the villages. This was the best time of the journey for soon we would eat something from the hamper, drink our tea from a flask, pull up the wooden slatted shutters and turn in to what must be the most evocative sounds of my childhood – the steam engine thundering into the Indian night and sounding its long drawn out wailing whistle.

My father had little financial resources other than his army pay but my mother belonged to a wide, embracing network of friends and relations and, with a small income of her own, we were able to rent bungalows at various hill stations or stay with some of her many friends. She always referred to these as her 'oofy' friends by which she meant they were wealthy or, at least, seemed to have much more money than we ever had. My favourite was the bungalow we returned to for a succession of years at the small hill station of Kasuli, between Chandigarh and Simla where, with its astonishing views, its luxuriant vegetation, its perpetually changing light and its clamorous insects and animals, I was captivated. In another year, we travelled to Rawalpindi and thence by road to Srinigar in Kashmir and to Gulmargh, a small circular plateau at about 8,000 feet reached only on horseback. There we stayed for some months in a smallish wooden house where my brother and I tried to chase the large brown apes which lurked in the fringing deodars whilst my mother spent her days playing golf or bridge. On Sundays, we would attend Sunday school in the little stone church set on a rise in the middle of the plateau in the middle of the golf course against the back-cloth of the Panyr range and Nanga Parbut.

After the Great War, India was in constant turmoil as national movements began to feel their strengths riding on a wave of discontent engendered by expectations of some measure of independence as a concession for India's participation in the war. There was the unfortunate massacre of nearly four hundred people at Amritsar in 1919 when the British, haunted by the spectre of the mutiny, brutally dispersed a nationalist gathering in an unprecedented show of armed force. The Rowlett Acts which gave the British Government unlimited powers against subversive organisations or persons, later sparked off a series of disorders and riots led by Mahatma Gandhi which was to culminate in the famous salt march in 1930.

Throughout this time, my father was often away on 'special duties' and we only saw him at intervals. For the first few years in India, he served as regimental officer with the Sikh Regiment but, by the time I was about to leave for England in 1930, we were alternating between Delhi and Simla as he moved backwards and forwards with army headquarters to which he had become attached as an intelligence and training officer. While my father's mind ranged over a wide spectrum of interests beyond the narrow confines of the Army, my mother was moulded in the lines of Anglo-India and her thoughts, as well as those of her family, were often dominated by the Mutiny. Even at that time, the Mutiny seemed to be ever present in the minds of many of the British as though it was a recent experience in which everyone had shared. And, at an official level, lines also led back to the Mutiny whereby the ration of Indian to British troops in each brigade and the class system which balanced recruitment into all Army units from elements unlikely by caste or religion to coalesce was rigidly maintained. As a child, I was only vaguely aware of these events and sometimes puzzled as to why some Indians seemed to dislike us whereas others, like our servants, were so loyal and kind and if I, as a child, found it puzzling, my elders were perhaps not much more enlightened as they stumbled and faltered trying to maintain a past which was already being blown away, all of them refusing to even contemplate the very thought of having to leave India one day.

As we sat there on that terrace, my father and I spoke, not of the past but of the future. Although he looked extremely fit, it came as a surprise when he said that he was in fact already too old for both his rank and active service and, when he had tried to inveigle himself into active service with the 4th Indian Division, in the Middle East, they had turned him down. He was now advising on the establishment of Ceylon's armed forces which he found to be a dismal task. He spoke of the Tamil and Singalese as being unlikely material for soldiering and thought the best they could do was possibly as pioneers or guards of military establishments but, even then, he had his doubts. In any event he was looking forward to returning to India within a month where he felt urgent tasks awaited him.

He was convinced that the war with Japan was inevitable and was depressed and disillusioned by Indian behaviour since the war had started. He felt that the Indian army was prepared to fight well anywhere at Britain's bidding but said that we should not be deceived into believing that this reflected the true feelings of the Indian people. The Indian army, he continued, had become a vast mercenary one under British tutelage and the closely-knit family affair of regiments of British officers and Indian men had almost divorced themselves from the seething affairs of the country. As my father talked on into the afternoon, stopping now and again to discuss my affairs and listening to my accounts, but always returning to the same subject. I was surprised at his views. He talked of the love-hate relationship between Britons and Indians and of India being like a vast country estate which we could now ill afford to keep up and, as far as Indian independence went, he felt that this could not be long delayed once the war was over but he abhorred the consequence and the collapse into anarchy which, in the event, would surely follow from Hindu-Muslim rivalry.

As we trundled along the darkening coast road back to Colombo, passing palm thatched huts and flickering coconut oil lamps fronting ubiquitous coconut plantations, he spoke of family affairs and, almost as if he had a premonition, advised me on his affairs and finances which did not actually amount to much. Then, in a sudden change of mood, he reverted to his natural good humour and we ended the journey by his recounting various recent experiences in humorous anecdote. He dropped me at the passenger jetty with cheerful admonitions to write to him and to look after myself. It was the last I ever saw of him.

In 1944, by which time he was a Lieutenant Colonel, upon rounding a bend in a jeep on a track somewhere near Imphal in Assam, he and his Ghurka escort were cut down in a hail of bullets from a Japanese ambush. He was then fifty-four and, by all accounts, had no business of being where he was which my mother saw as a betrayal of herself. She felt lonely and isolated at Kasauli. She soon recovered when my brother, Charles, then aged twenty, arrived in India with the RAF and was in Delhi for a while to where my mother had moved to live with her sister.

But all this was in the future and, as I stepped into the ship's launch, I felt a comfortable glow of pride and affection which continued when I returned to ship and where I basked callowly in the obvious interest of my brother midshipmen who all knew of the exchange of signals the previous day and my father's appearance on board earlier that day in the uniform of an Indian major.

On Saturday, November 29th at 17.00 hours, the Prince of Wales slipped and proceeded out of Colombo in company with the destroyers Electra, Express, Encounter and Jupiter through the swept channel and set course southward. Close range weapons were exercised. Early in the forenoon of the following day, the Prince of Wales and her escort joined up with the Repulse off the Little Basis islands which lie south eastwards of Ceylon. Force Z as the battle squadron was now known, set course for the Malacca Straits with the Repulse now leading the Prince of Wales in line ahead and the destroyers disposed as a screen.

We entered the Malacca Straits on the 1st of December, a hot, humid, overcast day and altered course to pass down through them to Singapore, entering the naval base in Johore Strait and secured against the West Wall opposite the dockyard main buildings and just ahead of the cruiser Mauritius. The Repulse anchored out in midstream.

Upon securing, Admiral Sir Tom Phillips, who had been promoted to full Admiral and appointed Commander-in-Chief, Eastern Fleet the previous day, immediately came on board with Rear Admiral Palliser, the short diminutive figure of the former contrasting strongly with the tall figure of the latter. On the day the Admiral had struck his flag in Colombo, he and his staff had flown straight to Singapore for urgent consultations in face of the rapidly deteriorating situation. Our arrival in Singapore also coincided with a declaration of emergency throughout Malaysia. Together with the local populace in Singapore, we felt that our arrival could not have been better timed and that our presence would provide the necessary deterrent to the Japanese. The local papers reported our arrival 'with other heavy units' and this had the effect of easing the feelings of vague apprehension which had built up within Singapore over the previous weeks. For ourselves, we believed that our arrival would in fact avert the threat of war and some looked forward to settling down to peacetime routine in exotic surroundings. There were, however, a number who opined that we would, after a month or two of showing the flag in such places as Hong Kong and Manila, return home.

HMS Prince of Wales arrives at Johore Naval Base, Singapore 1st Dec 1941

But whatever the future held for us all, we turned to a round of hard work during the day when I was given the additional task of helping an RNVR sub-lieutenant to amend a large pile of confidential books, known as cee-bees, but, on many afternoons, we were able to take a taxi into Singapore fifteen miles away. The city of Singapore was a handsome place with imposing buildings and a large open green on the sea front, the padang, flanked by the Supreme Court, a club, the imposing Anglican Cathedral and Raffles Hotel. Although hot, steamy and uncomfortable with daily thunder showers, it was the fulcrum of British power in the East, an impregnable fortress controlling the major seaway to the Far East. It also had a romantic allure and I was immediately and entirely enchanted. I had only recently read some of Somerset Maugham's short stories and my mind was filled with absurd and romantic notions of life for the Europeans in the Far East. Being then entirely impressionable and with little true perception, I had not noticed the irony in Maugham's writing and passed my days in complete fascination. Scapa Flow, the Home Fleet and the war all seemed part of another world, its desperate throes hardly nudging our minds. Even the Japanese seemed to have been comfortably disposed of by our very presence.

On the afternoon that I had spent with my father, he had given me a letter written on hotel note-paper to an old Indian army friend who now lived in Singapore. "Just in case you happen to fetch up there," he had said laconically as he handed it to me. Taking advantage of this, I eventually managed to phone his friend, Major France, who immediately invited me to meet him for drinks one evening at his home. This was a bungalow set in lush and exotic surroundings to the north of the city where he and his wife, plus dogs, led a comfortable and highly social life. Although somewhat younger than my father, Major France had known both him and my mother for years and was eager to hear news of them even though I had not seen my mother for years. He, in fact, had seen her more recently than I had. Mrs France was a small, neat person, good looking with very large blue eyes. I could see why my father was friendly with Major France for he was Anglo Irish with a clever, lean face, prominent lips and a low hair line which gave him the appearance of a leaner and more masculine Oscar Wilde.

He was also the antithesis of the Indian Army officer of popular caricature. When I met him, he seemed to be tired, drawn and agitated. He was much concerned with events and, although not disclosing his exact role in them, I remember him saying that while Singapore was impregnable, he was worried about the weaknesses inherent in the situation in Malaya where the population were probably subversive and communications poor enough to hamper an orthodox campaign, but one which could possibly favour the

61

Japanese who were well versed in rapid infiltration tactics. He had visited Japan in 1935 and, contrary to the blinkered thinking of the military in Singapore at the time, he seemed to have considerable respect for the Japanese army. And, as if to partly excuse the thinking of his colleagues, he also remarked that even if the Japanese were perhaps individually inferior soldiers, there was danger of us being overwhelmed by their sheer numbers. He nevertheless believed that a strong naval presence would have a deterrent effect upon Japanese designs, although he was not as complacent as some of us had become. He admonished me to read the history of the Russo-Japanese war and, in particular, how the Russian fleet, after having sailed half way round the world, was annihilated by the Japanese fleet under Admiral Togo at the battle of Tsushima in 1905.

With my complacency only mildly disturbed by the somewhat sombre outlook, I left him and his wife with an invitation to a dinner party the next evening, black tie she reminded me. I duly presented myself the next evening in a borrowed white mess jacket complete with black tie, cummerbund and black trousers. I was introduced to the other guests who were all colonial civil servants and their wives. The presence of civilians in the home of an army officer in those days was unusual at that time but it was a tribute to Major France's ability to move beyond the usual narrow confines of the military into the stratum of local society which generally had a strong antipathy to anyone in uniform. The meal was sumptuous, impeccably served under whirling fans and the conversation ranged mainly over local affairs. I was very young, somewhat flattered by the attention of my betters and, with a puppy like eagerness to please, my critical facilities were hardly developed. Had I been older, I may have perhaps detected an air of apprehension behind their bland, insular exterior but I did not and I was soon caught up in the happy, unconcerned atmosphere of the evening.

Perhaps they were not apprehensive at all because, after the war, the British civilians, no less the senior military command of Singapore were all severely criticised for their complacent attitude and lack of preparation. However, for a group who represented the privileged ruling class, it was inevitable that they would cling to the well-ordered routine of their lives, secure in their superiority. They were also all victims of the pervasive illusion of the strength of the Empire, the somewhat hollow boasting of the British Government on the strength of 'fortress Singapore', where millions had been spent on its naval base, the array of heavy coastal defence guns and the supposed inferiority of the Japanese which was based on racial concepts. The essential difference between the British at home and those in Singapore was, in the case of the former, the threat was recognised from earlier experience to be an impending contest between European equals whereas the latter behaved in many ways as privileged groups have done throughout history in the face of a revolution. For the impending conquest was, in essence, a Japanese led Asian revolution against all European rulers and it is not surprising therefore that feelings of racial superiority were responsible for the general air of unconcern and smugness. During the final days before the fall of Singapore, a well known story has it that the secretary of the golf course refused to allow a group of gunners to site their guns on the club greens without the prior consent of the committee – a ludicrous but understandable attempt to retain some vestige of order in a situation where the world was inexplicably collapsing all around them at the hands of 'those ridiculous people', the Japanese.

What made that evening even more memorable in retrospect was the fact that within just over forty-eight hours, Singapore would be bombed from the air and from that moment forwards, none of our lives would be the same again. I cannot remember the names of the other guests, nor do I know if they survived the war. Both Major France and his wife did, he emerging from Changi Prison in 1945 and she by boarding one of the last ships out of Singapore for India where I was to meet them both again.

Upon returning to the ship that night, I resolved to have a white mess jacket made for the pleasurable social round which I felt sure could only intensify. This idea was reinforced when I discovered that the Repulse and two destroyers had sailed, some said for Australia to show the flag over Christmas and the New Year. At this news, the somewhat vague fears planted by Major France subsided.

I remained on board on duty for most of the next day, Saturday. Late in the afternoon, whilst taking tea, the gunroom was suddenly agog with the news that the Japanese had invaded Siam and were headed towards Malaya in large convoys. The news was confused and based on an amalgam of vague news reports, rumours, speculation and some firm information gleaned from various quarters. On the other hand, that evening we listened to some midshipmen who had been to Singapore recount the sight of a vast Australian ceremonial parade which had taken place in Raffles Square that afternoon which hardly seemed consistent with Japanese moves towards Malaya. The next day however, Sunday, 7th of December, the Repulse returned to the base and this, combined with the continuing rumours, seemed to confirm that a general state of flap was now in progress. For many of us, the peaceful rounds of showing the flag, trips ashore and dinner parties was replaced by a new eagerness that, perhaps, after all, we would be closely involved in action within the next week at least. But nothing was certain because, by mid afternoon the 'buzz' had it that we were returning to the Home Fleet because the Japanese threat had subsided and the German battle cruisers, the Scharnhorst and Gneisenau were preparing for a break into the Atlantic. As it happened, this was uncannily, very nearly correct as these ships did break out three months later but not in the way we had assumed. Putting aside all these conflicting rumours, Errington and myself went ashore in the late afternoon to the Base swimming pool where we swam for a while and then sat talking to some of the Repulse midshipmen among whom were two Australians who complained bitterly at having been thwarted from the prospect of Christmas at home.

We turned in early that evening feeling relaxed and tired but, soon after 4a.m. I was jerked awake by the sound of the alarm rattlers and the urgent notes of the bugle calling all to 'Repel Aircraft stations'. At first I thought I was dreaming but suddenly I was awake and rapidly drawing on my clothes as other midshipmen turned out and some were already rushing to their action stations. I remember not being able to find my anti-flash gear but dashed off for the bridge without it. On emerging on to the deck, we heard the dockyard sirens wailing. Lights were going out everywhere and searchlights from the nearby Selatar airfield were probing the sky. As I reached the signal deck, I looked up and there, high in the sky were aircraft illuminated by searchlights and a bright half moon. At the same moment, our multiple pom-poms opened fire just below the signal deck and heavier anti-aircraft fire could be heard from ashore. The aircraft, which could only be Japanese, were very high and out of range of our pom-poms. Half the crew were still ashore and many of the communications to the directors and the secondary armament were unresponsive. The 'whump, whump' of our pom-poms was perhaps more comforting to our morale than they were effective and very soon came 'the order to 'Check, check, check.' We could now hear distant crumpling sounds as bombs exploded on Singapore City and to the east, near Solatar as I was being reprimanded by the Air Defence Officer for not having my anti-flash gear with me.

After the Japanese aircraft had droned away, we fell out from our action stations and all foregathered in the gunroom to discuss, with growing excitement, this sudden and latest development. Soon afterwards, someone came in with the startling news that the Japanese had landed in Malaya. This was confirmed later in the day with even more startling news. The Japanese had attacked the Americans in Pearl Harbour, almost knocking out her Pacific Fleet and also struck at Hong Kong and the Phillipines. Although we greeted this news with incredulity and outright disbelief, it was not without a quickening of the pulse and a renewed excitement.

Later the ship was brought to short notice for steam and manoeuvred away from the dock wall to give our secondary armament an improved field of fire should there be a recurrence of the raid. There was also a general signal, 'Commence hostilities against Japan'. All shore leave was cancelled and, at about lunch time, senior officers and captains of other ships within the base repaired aboard the Prince of Wales. Shortly afterwards the captains and officers left the ship and we were told that we would sail that afternoon.

We weighed and proceeded from the Naval Base at 17.00 hours and sailed down the Johore Strait in company with the Repulse. The destroyers Electra and Express were waiting outside the Strait, like a pair of faithful terriers waiting for their master, prior to setting out on a hunt. It was Monday, December the 8th. Once clear of the strait and off Changhi Point, the Vampire and Tenedos joined us. The Mauritius had been unable to sail due to engine trouble and three old D class cruisers, Durban, Danae and Dragon also remained behind presumably because they had been designed as patrol escorts and were ill fitted for battle fleet work.

17.00 hrs Mon 8th Dec 1941 HMS Prince of Wales

It was close to sunset when we sailed with the evening light growing hazy over Singapore Island, a slight breeze cooling the otherwise hot and heavy humid air. We proceeded slowly flapping the Admiral's flag, the cross of St. George, at the main mast above our white ensign. Once out of the strait, our bows lifting to the slow swell, we took station four cables ahead of the Repulse with the destroyers disposed on the screen. Earlier, the Repulse had led us out of the Strait and, when looking ahead from my harbour station on the bridge, her broad squat and low end-on profile viewed from astern looked remarkably like the Hood on her last voyage out of Scapa

Flow. The late evening light and the close proximity of the land on either side heightened the illusion and I felt a sudden feeling of uneasiness arising from an association of events. I had no premonition of disaster, merely a vague apprehension to what might befall the Repulse, not us. We were, after all, one of the world's most modern battleships and had already acquitted ourselves with some competence against the enemy. The Repulse, on the other hand, was twenty years old, lightly armoured, its anti aircraft armament of vintage standard and, despite an overfull share of sea-going time since the outbreak of war, had yet to fire her guns in anger. This did not, however, deter her crew from considering themselves one of the best ships' companies in the Royal Navy composed as it was of a very high proportion of regulars who tended to look down on the Prince of Wales's company who, in contrast, had a high proportion of 'hostilities only' ratings.

Soon after the order to darken ship, we went below to the stifling confines of the gunroom where later, at dinner, we listened to an address by the Gunnery Officer on the ship's broadcasting system. He told us that we had sailed with the objective of engaging the enemy and spoke of what could be expected. He mentioned that our opposition would probably be confined to the Old Japanese battleship, Kongo, and some cruisers, all of which did not add up to anything we felt we could not handle with our superior armament and speed. Our morale and excitement grew as we discussed among ourselves the possibility of a surface action from which we should surely emerge the victors. After all, we were all veterans and had already faced the Bismarck and the prospect of the Kongo which had been built in England in 1910 did not leave us at all dismayed.

After dinner some of us returned to the quarterdeck where we walked or talked in groups in the darkness. Other officers were also congregated in small groups. We all felt we would be in action shortly and spoke in excited tones at the prospect. Most of us remembered the first shock of battle and the awesome sight of the Hood blowing up and the deaths of our brother midshipmen but there was only a sharpening of the senses with little fear, most of us having only half emerged from immersion in the public school tradition which stood for militaristic heroism unimpaired by realism. Soon afterwards, I turned in. I had the middle watch from midnight to 4a.m. and it only seemed minutes later that I was being shaken by the midshipman of the watch. I was thankful to escape from the sweating confines between decks for the cooler breeze above. The night was moonlit and the sea calm as we maintained a north-easterly zig-zag course throughout the night.

With only a short respite below, I was again awakened around five o'clock to the ominous and somewhat mournful bugle notes of 'dawn action stations'. The sky lightened rapidly to a damp grey overcast and cloudy day with rain squalls in the offing as we maintained a North-easterly course at a speed of 18 knots to pass to the east of Anamba Islands. At about 7a.m. the force altered course to the north north-east and we stood down from action stations or 'second degree of readiness' but at 8a.m. was again back on watch at the air defence position. The horizon stayed clear as we steamed on through calm seas under an overcast but steamy sky. Shortly after mid-day, we altered course to the north to go round the Anamba Islands to the west. Apart from a patrolling Catalina flying boat which approached the force, our 271 air-warning radar detected no echoes within seventy to eighty miles. During the late afternoon, a general signal was sent to the fleet by Admiral Phillips.

This disclosed that the fleet was now heading into the entrance of the Gulf of Siam to intercept an enemy landing force which had been reported in the vicinity of Khota Bharu and our present course and speed should bring us to our targets just after first light the next day. It added that heavy Japanese surface units were known to be in the vicinity but, with our movements so far well concealed from the enemy, the element of surprise could prove to be decisive. It would soon be dark and we all felt confident, assured and, once again, that rising sense of excitement and the noise of one's heart beating was there. But, unbeknown to us, and a fact that I was only to discover many years later, we had been spotted by a Japanese submarine some hours before this signal had been sent. The crucial element of surprise had already been lost.

Just before sunset, the low, grey clouds broke up and the sun came out transforming the dull afternoon into a brilliantly clear, tropical evening. I had been below after my afternoon watch and came on deck to get some air and watch the sunset but, before many minutes had passed, the alarm rattlers sounded again and I was hurrying back to my action station. As soon as I reached the air defence position, I was told that a group of 'bogeys' (unidentified aircraft) had been detected on the radar and it was not long afterwards that an aircraft was sighted low on the horizon. It was soon identified as a ship-borne Japanese seaplane, obviously a shadower. It remained well out of range as a sinister portent on the horizon for some time before finally disappearing into the rapidly gathering dusk. I stood there contemplating its significance as it vanished in the evening light. Small in itself, it was now highly probable that we had been spotted, the element of surprise lost because it could only have come from either a battleship or heavy cruiser. Lending emphasis to my thoughts, it now seemed as though the ship itself was suddenly hushed in apprehension, there being no sound except the breaking of our bow wave in the slight swell against the general background hum of our ventilation exhausts as the sea darkened, the sky turned rapidly from green to amethyst to indigo and the foam of our wake began to glimmer with phosphorous.

An announcement was made saying that we would close-up to action stations again after darkness and would remain so throughout the night. We were then stood down to enable us to snatch a meal and change into action clothing. Since leaving Mauritius on our outward journey, we had dressed in tropical rig of shirt, shorts and stockings except when ashore at nights when we were required to dress in our no. 10 uniforms, the long, white trousers and choker-necked tunics. There were a few midshipmen eating a hurried scratch meal in the gunroom in a dim, yellowish light giving the now stripped space an empty, gloomy appearance. I managed to make a sandwich from what was spread out at the end of the table and then retired to change into clean underwear, long trousers and a long sleeved shirt. Errington was with me and we spoke in a low, hushed undertone, almost as if the Japanese could hear us. He seemed much more aware of the danger in which we now found ourselves than I was and I can remember him talking about the lack of an aircraft carrier, reminding me how easy it had been for the Italians to torpedo the Nelson during our brief sortie in the Mediterranean a few months previously and how easily the Japanese had almost annihilated the American Fleet at Pearl Harbour within the last forty-eight hours if what we had heard so far was true.

At 18.45 hours, hands closed up to action stations and, at 19.00 hours the course was altered to the north-west and the speed increased to 25 knots. It was Tuesday, December the 9th. We were now heading directly into the Gulf of Siam and the increased frequency of vibration tended to heighten the sense of urgency of our task. Perhaps we would gain some advantage by arriving off the invasion area in the hours of darkness even if we had been spotted. Soon after we had steadied on our new course, the entire Force made an emergency turn to port after the Electra reported sighting a flare in the sky ahead. We were all now alert for this could only mean a searching aircraft or perhaps a star-shell fired from a surface ship but, as the minutes ticked slowly by, there was no further word and our radar screens remained clear.

Then, at about 8pm, the ship altered course away southwards and speed was reduced to the original 18 knots. None of us were, of course, privy to what was going through the Admiral's mind but there was now a feeling of disappointment and anti-climax. It almost seemed that we had charged ahead impulsively only to be frightened off at the first sign of the enemy and our only consolation was that we were now retiring at high speed. Some of us assumed that some intelligence had come to hand and we settled down for the night to await developments but disappointment soon spread. I heard one of the ratings say to another, "We're just as bad as the bloody Ities, one whiff of the enemy and we're off. What a bloody shower." I pretended I hadn't heard but one of the lieutenants, a Canadian, had and he rounded on the rating telling him to pipe down. Unbeknown to us, our sortie was already bordering on the reckless as we were now steaming in an area thick with Japanese ships and aircraft who

70

were at that moment, frantically searching for us over these dark, tepid waters.

Another hour of silent waiting went by during which time, I was sent off to make cocoa for the other officers but which I found I couldn't drink myself in the heavy, humid and hot air. But tradition dies hard. The Navy had always drunk cocoa on the night watches and the fact that we were only a few miles north of the Equator made no difference. Some of the seamen were more enterprising because one of them soon appeared with a fanny full of cold cordial, a sweetened drink from the canteen known as 'goffers' a term whose derivation I never did find out. I was offered an enamel mug of goffers by one of the seamen. Shortly afterwards, a general signal was sent by the Admiral to the Force saying the intended operation had been cancelled and we were now heading southwards and returning to Singapore.

Our initial disappointment and sense of anti-climax on hearing this was gradually replaced by a sense of relief. One of the lieutenants said that the decision to call the operation off was based on the supposition that, as we had been spotted by the Japanese that evening, it was most unlikely that we would find a target in the morning. There was also the added danger that we may have been led into a trap in confined waters ranged by the Japanese flown over by Japanese shore-based aircraft. With this announcement, the ship reverted to defence station and those not required were told to rest close by. I was now profoundly tired. My eyes felt as though they had large pieces of grit in them. The lack of sleep, the increasing tension throughout the day, the sinister game of hide and seek we seemed to be playing with the Japanese, rising expectations and a sense of anti-climax now all combined into a great weariness within me. I found a quiet spot near the air defence position and was soon huddled and fast asleep.

Some time in the middle of the night, I was awakened by a sudden increase in vibration as we increased speed. I went off to try and find out what was happening and, by chance, met Errington who was on his way back to his action station at the starboard oerlikens. He told me that we had turned south-westwards towards the coast of

Malaya where the Japanese had made a new landing. I did not know what to make of this except a new excitement and began to feel confident and wide awake but there was still nothing to do as the ship remained at defence stations and moved through a now moonlit night towards the coast of Malaya.

Food was brought to those on watch an hour before dawn. Others went below to find what they could and then came the low notes of the bugle calling everyone to action stations. The early morning air was damp and cool with a slight offshore breeze and, as the sky lightened, I thought I could smell the tropical odours of land, which was probably only imagined because land was still some 60 miles away to the south west. For the next few hours we sailed through a calm, blue sea with a gentle swell while the sun climbed into the eastern sky behind us warming our backs. There was, however, nothing to disturb the peaceful morning as we all swept the horizon with our glasses which was already becoming diffused in the heat haze. Suddenly there was a report of an aircraft shadowing us, another snooper, and soon we could make out a tiny black dot, low on the eastern horizon, moving backwards and forwards in a pre-set pattern, watching us.

After some time, it disappeared and, once again, I was filled with a sense of foreboding. I was reminded of boyhood tales of Red Indians flitting through the undergrowth, scouting the ground as a prelude to attack. For me, at least, these shadowers were quite unnerving to observe and my mind was filled with questions – who were they? Were they now getting off a sighting signal? Soon afterwards, our own Walrus amphibian aircraft was catapulted off and we all watched it fly towards the coast, waddling through the air like some slow moving domestic duck which had inexplicably managed to fly.

Land was sighted ahead at eight o'clock, a low, greenish-blue line on the horizon and, as we drew closer, we could make out nothing except a long green line of jungle which seemed to reach down to the sea, with only the odd flash of white water betraying breaking surf. No ships were seen and everything seemed as silent as the grave under the torpor of the tropical sun as the Repulse and ourselves reduced speed and turned south-eastwards to run parallel to the coast. The Express was detached and could be seen increasing speed towards Kuantan Harbour which was merely a small cluster of buildings breaking the monotony of the green jungle. As I watched through my glasses, I wondered what had become of our Walrus for it had not returned. It was only later that I discovered it had already sent a message to say that Kuantan was clear of ships and had gone on to land at Selatar Airfield in Singapore. Soon the Express was flashing a signal with her large, blue, distant signalling lamp to say that Kuantan was all quiet, thus confirming the report from the Walrus, whereupon the Force turned away, increased speed and soon the coast was rapidly receding astern in a blue haze.

There was an almost immediate feeling of relief, but one of eeriness as well as we sped away from the coast and reverted to defence watches once again. I was ravenous and immediately made for the gunroom where I found the stewards had already returned from their action stations in the magazines and breakfast was being served. I remember eating a large breakfast of fried bread, tinned tomatoes and bacon with lots of tea before going off to have a shower. The midshipmen's bathroom was a large, tiled space with numerous baths and showers. When I got there, many others were there with similar ideas to my own. There was high spirited horse-play as some slid around on the slippery floor but the bathroom was not a place to linger as it was stifling hot and steamy with the spray from the showers. Soon a group of us were back on the quarter deck, re-dressed in our action clothes and sitting on ventilator outlets talking and smoking and relaxing in the hot sunshine.

There was some uneasy speculation as it seemed we were now headed north eastwards again, almost reversing our course of the latter part of the night. Soon we were joined by Errington who, as usual, seemed to have all the latest information. This time he jolted us all by saying that he had just heard that the Tenedos, one of the destroyers detached the previous night to return to Singapore, had been bombed by Japanese aircraft a short while ago to the southward. I remember being alarmed at this news because it meant that Japanese aircraft were ranging over the sea between ourselves and

Singapore and, somehow, I sensed that a trap was about to be sprung on us. As this news seemed to be full of urgent foreboding, we all dispersed and I went back to the bridge area to be close at hand should action stations be sounded again. I went to the signal deck and joined in conversation with Yeoman of Signals, Platt, one of the Yeomen who took us for signal instruction each morning. As we stood in the starboard side of the signal deck, he told me that an aircraft had been sighted a few minutes earlier to the south, another shadower, and that we had altered course to the east.

This was the third time that we had been spotted by a shadower and, coupled with the news of the bombing of the Tenedos, I now began to feel decidedly apprehensive and betrayed and said as much to Platt, whom I found to be as unnerved as I was at the continued sighting of Japanese aircraft watching us from a distance. He added that he, 'wished to God they would get on with it', and I had to agree that anything was better than this sinister game of hide-and-seek. While we all watched and waited with a subdued tension, nothing disturbed the hot, clear day except another report that a British merchantman had been sighted on a southward course for Singapore. I remember finding this somehow incongruously comic. There we were, a powerful British naval force heading eastward, being menacingly shadowed by Japanese scouting aircraft and a small merchantman plodding past with all the unconcern of someone going about his mundane work, entirely unimpressed with the British Navy swanking nearby. In truth, however, her captain was probably very alarmed and doing his best to get out of the way as soon as possible.

It was Wednesday, December 10th and radar detected echoes of a large formation of approaching aircraft 45 miles away to the east and the ship closed-up to Repel Aircraft stations.

As the last of the bugle's urgent notes died away which seemed to say, 'There's a bomber overhead, there's a bomber overhead', I was already on the air defence position. Lookouts were straining towards the horizon for the first sight of aircraft and our two large battle ensigns were hoisted at the fore and main. Lines of communication were tested, each turret reporting 'closed up' while the secondary armament direction began to traverse, searching the

74

sky ahead. After all this time, we were ready, as ready as we would ever be after our long journey almost half way round the world.

At about 11am nine aircraft were sighted ahead on the starboard bow in a tight formation, very high and glinting in the sun. Orders from the air defence position were soon passed to 'open fire' and in the director information on range, direction and height was passed to the 'Plot' well down in the bowels of the ship where it was fed into a calculator, the fore-runner of the computer, from which fuze setting was instantly transmitted to the guns. When the guns were loaded, a hooter sounded in the director which were then fired by trigger as soon as the fuze settings coincided with the range. All eight starboard 5.25s now began firing in controlled salvoes at the aircraft as the ship swung in the same direction in response to an emergency turn to starboard and the sky ahead was filled with bursting shells but well away from the approaching aircraft. I remember thinking at the time that something drastic had gone wrong but only realised later that it was because we were simultaneously swinging to starboard that our bursts were being thrown to the right. The starboard 5.25.s now ceased firing as the arc or fire closed and the port battery opened fire, but none of this seemed to have the slightest effect on the Japanese planes who flew steadily towards us. As the turn to starboard was checked, we began to swing back to port and the whole ship began to judder in response to the increased revolutions. Soon the 5.25.s were able to bear and began firing in rapid salvoes but, by this time, the Japanese aircraft were almost overhead and seemed to have lost height. We all stared with a terrified fascination as they flew almost directly over us as we expected to be showered by bombs at any moment. But they maintained their course and flew on and we then saw sticks of bombs falling on the Repulse. Almost immediately, the Repulse, now fine on our starboard quarter, was engulfed in towering spouts of water as the bombs hit the sea. At this, the vague apprehension I had felt as we left Singapore came back to me and I thought, 'My God, it is the Hood again.' I expected to see the Repulse, her half sister ship, explode and collapse into the sea. But she soon emerged from the shower of falling water unscathed except for some black smoke arising from amidships.

The Japanese aircraft rapidly disappeared and, except for black smoke indicating that at least one bomb had struck her, there was nothing else to indicate that anything untoward had happened during the past fifteen minutes. Some of us were jubilant and tended to deride the Japanese bomb aiming. All those bombs and only one hit. My high spirits were, however short lived as I began to think of our lack of air cover and how easy it would have been had there been a squadron of Hurricanes over our heads. The Japanese, flying in close formation at a steady height would have fallen easy victims to fighters attacking from above them and out of the sun. Although more than a dozen salvoes had been fired, no hits were made. Once again, my mind went back to Admiral Holland's handling of the Hood and the Prince of Wales in those last moments of his life six months ago which prevented us from initially bringing all our guns to bear on the Bismarck. Similarly, we had again been prevented from bringing sustained fire to bear by a manoeuvre which, in retrospect, was the exact opposite to what should have been ordered. Had Admiral Phillips sustained our initial move to port and, thus presented a narrow target to aircraft approaching on the beam, we could have kept up a sustained barrage which may well have resulted in the downing of a few aircraft and perhaps deter the aim of the others.

Now, in the relative silence of the sky and the sea, we all knew that the Japanese would be back. It was still a long way to the time of darkness, sufficient for them to return with another load of bombs or, worse, with a larger force now that they knew precisely where we were. Our fears were soon realised when, after about ten minutes, our radar detected another large formation of aircraft, ten plus it was reported, but now approaching us from the unexpected direction of the south east.

At 11.40 hours, two separate groups of twin-engined bombers were sighted approaching from the south west flying in two formations at about ten thousand feet.

We were soon tracking the formation on the air defence position as it flew just out of range along the eastern horizon where it split into two groups, the larger continuing across our bows and the other swinging away southward again. As we watched, the first group began to lose height rapidly in line ahead as they flew across our bows to our port side where they wheeled towards us in three separate groups of three. There was no sound as we watched, almost mesmerised into helplessness by the precision of the manoeuvre. Now the aircraft turned towards us seeming to lose more height until, they were flying fast at about a hundred feet and boring straight for us. The seconds ticked away as we watched tensely with our 5.25.s and all close range weapons trained and ready to fire. The range closed rapidly but there seemed to be a long delay in opening fire and I went through agonising seconds silently saying to myself, 'Open fire. For Christ's sake, open fire.'

Finally the 5.25.s commenced firing with their distinctive crack followed by the pom-poms and the oerlikens and shrouding the whole port side with cordite smoke. The sky was punctured with the black bursts of our exploded 5.25.s around the aircraft and the sea beneath boiled in a froth as the shrapnel hit the water. But the Japanese came on without wavering and I had a sudden fear that they were either trying to bomb us at low level or crash into us in some cataclysmic suicide attack. The 5.25.s now switched to barrage fire throwing a curtain of exploding projectiles ahead of the rapidly closing aircraft but, miraculously, they flew through it all. Lookouts reported torpedoes being dropped and soon their tracks could be seen but I saw neither, conscious only of the ship turning to port as I fixed my eyes on the aircraft still flying straight at the ship. Suddenly I was aware of explosive sounds all around me and large pieces of paintwork flying around and, within seconds, large twin-engined aircraft passed over us showing their underbellies. Some said afterwards that they could see the faces of the Japanese crews looking down on us as they passed over. I did not but I do not doubt their words. They were very close.

All our attention was now fixed on the tracks of the torpedoes as they sped towards us whilst the ship swung in an effort to comb their tracks but, before we were able to do so, there came a shattering explosion followed by terrific banging and jolting on our port quarter where a column of brackish-white water rose well above us.

Although expecting to be hit by a torpedo, my mind hardly registered that we had in fact been hit by at least one. I was conscious only of a gigantic shock wave which seemed to pass through the entire ship, followed by a strange whiplash vibration as though the ship's engines had sprung their mountings and were running loose in the engine room. Soon this vibration ceased and the ship began to lose way and, almost immediately, we had a list to port.

Then came the reports that the second group of aircraft which, earlier, had broken away from the initial formation, were preparing to attack the Repulse who was now turning at speed under full helm some distance on the starboard side. Following on this, there were lookouts reports that a further formation of high level bombers were also approaching the Repulse. Exactly what was happening was not clear to me and I remember seeing only huge columns of water rising all around her, similar to the bomb explosions of the previous day. At intervals our starboard 5.25.s briefly aimed at aircraft overshooting their attacks on the Repulse but, for the present, most of us turned our attention to ourselves as it was clear that we had been grievously damaged. All communication with the after secondary armament went dead and we received verbal reports of the after 5.25. inch magazines having been flooded. The forward 5.25.s were also unable to train as all power had failed. One of the engine rooms had been put out of action, the main steering gear immobilised and the ventilation system ceased to function which must have made life below almost intolerable. I also discovered that a number of men had been killed on the signal deck just below us by machine gun fire from the aircraft as they passed over. Two Japanese aircraft were said to have been shot down, crashing into the sea on our disengaged starboard side but I did not see this.

At 12.10 hours, the Prince of Wales hoisted, 'Not under control.'

The last attack on the Repulse ended at about noon. There was now a lull as we wallowed at about 15 knots completely out of control whilst the Repulse could be seen closing us on the starboard side. Seeing the two black balls on the yard-arm, which signified that we were out of control, I felt my confidence beginning to wane. As reports came through from the eight separate twin 5.25 turrets, it was clear that there were defects of various kinds in all of them although determined efforts were being made to bring them back into operation. Not only were we unable to steam at speed or manoeuvre but we were suddenly incapable of defending ourselves against aircraft. The close range weapons, particularly the pom-poms, had also suffered defects from ammunition supplies where the electric hoists had failed. But surprisingly, apart from the ten degree list to port, there was no outward sign of damage. Until then, we had only suffered a few upper deck casualties. The real damage was deep in our vitals where the damage control parties and engineers were apparently struggling to restore power and control, unseen by those of us on the upper deck.

With the possibility now beginning to nudge the corner of my mind that we might sink, even without further attacks which were sure to materialise, I remembered with some disappointment that I had left my money in my chest down below. This amounted to about £20 which was the equivalent of two month's pay. I now realised the advantage of keeping money in condoms which were issued free from the sick bay and were often put to other uses than those for which they were intended. We had even heard of one armed trawler whose cat had been issued with a life belt devised from an inflated condom attached to its collar.

Now, after the lull had lasted for just over a quarter of an hour, lookouts reported a large formation of aircraft, about twice as many as before, approaching from the east and, once again, we watched them split into two formations and lose height. Real fear now gripped me as this was obviously the coup-de-grace for us as we moved slowly, barely functioning with all our guns, except the two for'ard starboard 5.25. turrets, out of action. As the attack developed, it was clear that the Japanese had changed their tactics. There now seemed to be aircraft approaching from several angles. The aircraft also seemed to be of a larger and different type to those of the earlier attacks but there was no mistaking their intention as they closed rapidly on the starboard side at varying heights. The two remaining 5.25.s fired a number of salvoes but, as the aircraft flew closer and lower, they were unable to depress the guns sufficiently enough owing to the list to port. Close range weapons joined in but none of this fire seemed to deter the Japanese and, within seconds, they were breaking away over us having dropped their torpedoes. On this occasion I did see the tracks of at least two torpedoes speeding directly towards us. But now, there was no possibility of turning to comb their tracks. We were a perfect, wallowing, listing target.

The torpedoes, not two but four, struck with shattering explosions in quick succession when the whole ship seemed to lift out of the water and move sideways as huge columns of water rose up around us. One of the torpedoes seemed to have struck directly under the bridge and another, just abaft the superstructure. When the spray cleared, I could see the Repulse just ahead of us on the starboard beam and turning with, what seemed to be, at least six aircraft flying with her at varying heights and then, momentarily, two balls of fire as two of them fell in flames into the sea off her bows. Almost immediately, I noticed that the Repulse was listing to port and I could see more and more of her upper deck as her list increased alarmingly. My attention was distracted at that moment and, when I looked again, the Repulse was unbelievingly heeling over as the two escorting destroyers moved to stand by her.

Eight aircraft flying in close formation at about 10,000 feet, approached us fine on the port bow and the warning klaxon on the bridge was sounded once again. By this time, the listing had been counterbalanced by the flooding from the torpedo hits on the starboard side and all the forward 5.25.s were thus able to come back into action on a level platform. As the aircraft droned on towards us, the 5.25.s opened fire and this time their aim was good and bursts were seen to be close to the aircraft but, nevertheless, without affecting their steady onward flight. Within minutes they were over our bows and began releasing their bombs. The Air Defence Officer shouted, "Take cover," and we dived for cover in a confusion of legs, arms, telephone leads and steel helmets. There was not much cover but I crouched and flattened myself as close as I could to the parapet. After what seemed to be a long time, as we held our breaths, there was the most terrific explosion just abaft of us, almost knocking us senseless and accompanied by what sounded like a great tearing of metal. Almost immediately, we were completely enveloped in black, hot, breath-searing smoke. We quickly recovered and returned to our head-sets and telephones but everything now seemed to be dead and lifeless. The bombs had struck us amidships in the catapult deck and, from all accounts, had penetrated deep into the ship. It was at this instant that many of the 300 men who were to die on that day, were killed. I heard later that this bomb had penetrated into the cinema flat which was then being used as a casualty station and was packed with wounded and exhausted men. The whole of the mid-ship section below decks had apparently been reduced to a bloody shambles from blast, flash and flying metal in less than a minute.

When the smoke cleared, there was almost complete silence. I realised that the Prince of Wales was no longer underway and we were now stopped dead in the water. No longer was there a roar of ventilation from the funnel and I could hear the sea lapping against the side. I looked to see if I could see the Repulse but there was no sign of her. It did not occur to me that she had already sunk, which she had, a good ten minutes before while our attention had been focused on the approaching, final wave of aircraft. We were also, by this time, settling by the stern as one of the destroyers, the faithful Express, approached us close to on our starboard quarter. As we settled deeper into the water, Carley floats were being thrown from the quarter-deck and the Express began taking off men from just abaft of the catapult deck. There was nothing more for any of us to do although, incredibly, some of our telephones were working again and the lookouts were still searching the skies for more Japanese planes. I felt terribly lethargic and everything took on a dream-like quality, my mind refusing to believe that the ship was actually sinking. Some of the men were told to fall out and make their way below. The Air Defence Officer looked at me for a moment and said, "You too, Mid, carry on." Without further urging, I saluted and dashed off below. None of those who remained in the Air Defence position survived.

As I descended the bridge structure, the ship took a sudden lurch and the list to port began to increase at what seemed to be an alarming rate. On making my way along the starboard side, everything was a complete shambles and shrouded in this acrid smoke. There were empty ammunition cases, mangled steel, clothing, lifebelts and, incongruously, a marine's red-banded white cap stuck on a stanchion. I began to hurry and clambered up a ladder to the S3 5.25 mounting, the deck littered with empty shell cases, and then down on to the quarterdeck. I then noticed that the port side of the quarterdeck was almost awash and I could see the Express rapidly moving astern about three cables away. There was also, by this time, a large group of men standing on the starboard side of the quarterdeck where some were letting themselves down on ropes into the water but, as the list increased, the starboard side began to rise and the sea looked further and further away.

I stood there for some time completely frozen by indecision. I was a fairly strong swimmer but, to go over the starboard side with the sea now glistening with oil, with the danger of breaking a limb was a frightening option but, the port side, now nearly awash, seemed infinitely more perilous where I feared being sucked under or, even worse, have the ship roll over on top of me. However my mind was soon made up for me by a burly marine who grabbed me and said, "Come on, lad," and, without further ado, we both went sliding down the starboard side in a sitting position at an incredible speed to hit the water feet first, just missing the end of a thick, armour-plating belt. Unfortunately, I hit a spar of wood that rose up and hit me across the head and eyes. As I surfaced, I put my hands up to my face as I found I was momentarily blinded by the blow but I could feel two strong arms gripping me and, gradually, I began to see through half closed eyes. I was also aware of a stinging sensation in my buttocks as the salt water seeped into the abrasions of that high speed slide and I then realised that the seat of my thin trousers had worn through.

The sea was warm and calm but there was a thick layer of fuel oil everywhere and those around me had black faces with only the whites of their eyes, red gums and teeth clearly visible. Soon after we entered the sea, a low flying fighter with British markings swooped over us which was greeted by derisive cries from the few men next to us and by the marine who was now swimming alongside me and who shouted, "Bloody Brylcream boys. Where were you?" We were swimming towards a Carley float when I looked back towards the Prince of Wales which, at that instant, was sinking, her bows rearing out of the water as she slid, upside down and stern first into the sea with a crashing, rumbling sound. Then, with an awesome swiftness, there was nothing but men, wreckage, Carley floats and the Express slowly moving through the water picking up survivors and, some distance away, two more destroyers picking up survivors from the Repulse.

After a slow breast stroke, I reached the Carley float which was full of men with no room for any additional survivors. I had to cling to a life-line. Once again, I looked back to where I had last seen the Prince of Wales and there was nothing but I felt no emotion, merely a thankfulness at having survived and disbelief of what I had witnessed. My mind went back to that day, seven months ago when I joined the Prince of Wales in Scapa Flow and being overawed by her sheer size, implied power and invincibility. It was inconceivable that I should now be swimming away from her as she slid into the sea but soon these thoughts were thrust away by the more immediate sight of a dead man floating past on his stomach, his head under water and his blue, inflated lifebelt standing up from his mid-riff.

After some time, the men in the Carley float started to regain their spirits and there was much dry comment and derisive laughter. A number of men began to sing and the words came floating over the water.

> "I don't want to join the navy,
> I don't want to go to sea,
> I'd rather hang around
> Piccadilly underground
> And live on the earnings
> Of a high-born lady.

A rating next to me started to tell me that all this had been told to him by a Chinese fortune teller that he had consulted in Singapore a few days earlier. I began to take note of what he was saying because many of us thought there was something sinister in the way the Japanese had found us so easily with their shore based aircraft. I also knew that it was strictly forbidden for servicemen to consult fortune tellers but I didn't say so. In retrospect, all this was harmless enough as the Chinese in Singapore were probably more realistic about the Japanese abilities than we were.

After about half an hour, during which time I was becoming increasingly nauseated because I had ingested a large amount of oil, the Express drew alongside and we were hauled aboard, some scrambling up the nets and others were hauled up on ropes. By this time, the decks were completely filled with men and there was hardly room to move. Someone thrust a mug of hot rum into my hands and, after the first few gulps, I was violently ill. The man next to me kept saying, "That's it son, puke it all up." I noticed that it was all brown oil that I was bringing up. After an interval, I began to feel much better. Someone else gave me a cigarette which, after inhaling, caused me to gag and vomit once more over the side of the ship. After picking up more men, the Express parted company with the Electra and Vampire who remained to pick up the remaining survivors. There were a thousand survivors from the Prince of Wales on board. Her normal complement was about 145. Had there been a sea running, it would have been impossible for her to retain stability with what must have been an additional seventy tons of weight.

Having recovered somewhat from the effects of swallowing the oil, I tried to move around to see if I could find any other midshipmen. I was dressed only in an oil soaked shirt and long trousers and, as I had no badges of rank nor my cap, I was taken for a boy seaman by some who told me to mind my manners as I tried to push past. I was overjoyed to find Errington sitting on the torpedo tubes amidships and abaft the funnel with two other midshipmen. He was almost unrecognisable, oil-begrimed and soaked but, incredibly still wearing his cap. At first we were all rather off-hand with each other as if being sunk was an every day part of our training but, gradually, we began to exchange experiences with each other. Although I had had a good vantage point during the battle, I was amazed to learn how much I had missed and soon there was an

84

argument about how many aircraft we had shot down – some said two, others said four. We all agreed however that someone had let us down for we knew that we were much nearer to our air bases in Malaya and Singapore than the Japanese airfields in Indo-China, or were the Japanese already operating from bases in Malaya. When we left the scene, only three hours had elapsed since we had opened fire on the first wave of bombers although it seemed that we had been in action all day. We now settled down to the eight or nine hour voyage back to Singapore with a chill sense of abandonment and foreboding, even betrayal as darkness fell upon the South China Sea.

Last moments of the Prince of Wales. Survivors transferring to GMS Express about 13.15hrs Wed 10th Dec 1941

Soon afterwards, we passed four American destroyers heading north and we watched signals being exchanged as they maintained a northwards course. Although, by this time, I was exhausted from lack of sleep, I found myself becoming more bright-eyed with nervous tension and lack of sleep as the hours wore on. I think I was also a little drunk. Later, one of the Express crew handed us some clothing and I gained a pair of white duck trousers which fitted me perfectly. He also gave me a pair of plimsolls which did not.

It seemed only a short time later that we hove to at the entrance to Johore Strait, the land showing darkly to the north with the glimmer of a few lights from Changhi Point on Singapore Island. By about 11p.m. we were edging our way alongside the dock wall of the naval base and soon we were all filing ashore. By this time, I had developed a delayed head-ache, possibly from too much rum, although I noticed that some men were very definitely drunk and given to passing loud remarks to anyone who cared to listen. Many of the men were without shoes and were soon hobbling across the gravel behind the dock wall, some were being carried on others' backs and there were many on stretchers. There was also a large number of seamen from other ships all ready to give a hand. Two of them, in immaculate white asked me if I wanted a hand as I shuffled along in my too small plimsolls, the backs of which I had folded down and used them as slippers.

The dockyard staff had set up bright arc light and trestle tables and we were all asked to form a line and give our name and rank to a Paymaster Officer. Writers were busily filling in forms behind the tables. The bright light seemed to cast a deathly pallor over the whole scene. The Prince of Wales crew looked a motley lot. Some had no shoes. There were some without trousers and many without shirts. A number were wrapped in blankets. Most had oiled streaked faces and what clothes were being worn were already beginning to give off a pungent, sour, nauseating odour of fuel oil in the humid night air. In retrospect, it was an ignominious sight and full of pathos, the pathetic human flotsam from a once proud 35,000 ton battleship embodying all the traditions and skill of British shipbuilding made a mockery of by some modern iconoclasts who, less than a hundred years before, were pursuing a life of feudal isolation. However, at the time, I felt none of this. In fact I remember being rather precocious and tiresome with some of those who had remained in Singapore. We had actually been in action with the Japanese and, being a survivor, added a certain cachet to our standing. The young are sometimes both callous and insensitive but perhaps this is merely a protective reflex because, after a hot shower, a meal and dead sleep for many hours, reaction set in.

When I woke the next morning, my head ached, my hands shook. I felt feverish ill and quite bewildered. Fuel oil seemed to have permeated my whole body and its pungency nauseated me. I was sharing a room with Errington and others and I felt worse as we walked to the parade ground - one of the seven football pitches within the base. I was now dressed in white overalls and had shoes that fitted. We were to be addressed by Captain Tenant of the Repulse and the new Commander in Chief, Admiral Layton. Neither Admiral Phillips nor Captain Leach had survived. The survivors of both ships were on parade, about two thousand men from an entire complement of three thousand drawn up in two groups. I was surprised to see how many of the Repulse's men had survived after her comparatively swift sinking. Captain Tenant made a cheering and rousing speech and promised his utmost that we all got survivor's leave and, if possible, at home in England. In contrast, Admiral Layton told us that the majority of us would remain in the east and that he would shortly be leaving Singapore for Ceylon from where strong naval forces would be assembled to return to avenge our losses. Upon being dismissed, there was wry comment because, to the average seaman, this was interpreted as 'Up the ladder, Jack, I'm alright.' Years later, I was to remember that Admiral Layton didn't actually say when this strong naval force would return. In fact is was to be just a few months short of four years before Singapore would again see the return of a strong, British naval force.

The senior surviving officer was the first Lieutenant, Lt Commander Skipwith, and it fell to him to co-ordinate the writing of reports of both officers and men while events were still fresh in our minds. We were issued with new journals and instructed to write the events of the past week but, as I began to contemplate the empty pages in front of me, I began to perspire and tears filled my eyes. Words alone seemed quite inadequate.

The writing of our accounts provided a form of cathartics to the events of that week and we soon began to unwind and relax. Some of us were now allowed out of the base. Errington and I went into

87

Singapore on the Saturday afternoon and instructed the taxi to take us straight to the France's house. Even though we arrived unannounced, we were given a relieved welcome by both of them as I introduced Errington. The news of our sinking had only just been announced a day or so before and Mrs France kept saying that she had been anxiously awaiting any news of me and she had been terribly worried and somewhat illogically, "What was I to tell your parents when I saw them again if anything had happened to you?"

As we sat and enjoyed a traditional afternoon tea of cakes and sandwiches, we talked about our experience, each one taking over when the other grew tired.

Major France listened intently to everything we said and soon we were listening to his account of the latest news from the Siam-Malaya border area where things were not going well and it seemed, as he had predicted, that the Japanese were moving fast by rapid infiltration tactics, leaving our own men, British, Australian and Indian, bewildered and frequently cut off. There was insufficient air cover for Singapore and the recent raids had been carried out almost with impunity. Although a realist, he was also an optimist and opined that once we had consolidated a line across the Malayan peninsula, the Japanese would be held and Singapore would soon be built up with the imminent arrival of aircraft and fresh divisions of troops from England that were now on their way. He enjoined us not to speak freely of what he had said suddenly aware, perhaps, that he was breaking security regulations and went on to talk about the changes that had overtaken the normal, everyday relationship between the local populace and the Europeans. There had been demands for outrageous increases in pay and many had simply disappeared across the Johore causeway northward to be lost in the thousands of kampongs of Malaya. At the same time, many Europeans had started a reverse migration from up-country seeking safety and sanctuary in Singapore, despite the danger of air attacks, whereby the city became more and more crowded until its population had almost doubled. Despite the evidence of continued Japanese successes in Malaya, people nevertheless planned for the forthcoming Christmas and New Year holidays, flocked to Raffles to dance, to the Adelphi where another band performed nightly and to films at Alhambra.

We lingered on at the Frances' and were persuaded to stay on for dinner. We were reluctant to do so as we were dressed in tropical rig of shorts and shirts which could not be worn ashore after dark. The correct rig was our no. 10 uniform which we no longer possessed but we were reassured by Major France who said he was sure we would not get into trouble. This was a vain hope. As we entered the Naval Base later that night, the Officer of the Watch, a RNVR lieutenant, happened to see us and we were both given a bottle for being out of rig of the day. When I tried to trade on our status as survivors, he remained unimpressed and said that we should have arranged for a tailor to run up a few sets for us. "After all," he said, "they only take a day or two in town."

We both walked off smarting with Errington muttering with all the force of an experienced eighteen year old about 'bloody shore-based wallahs.'

A few days later, seven of us midshipmen, including myself, were told that we would be joining the Exeter, an 8 inch gun cruiser which had arrived in Singapore on the day that we were sunk. She was tied up alongside in our former berth. We were all immeasurably cheered by this news and looked forward to an escape from a pervasive air of ill feeling which had quickly spread among the survivors. Some had already been drafted to other ships on the station and a favoured fifty per cent had been selected for passage home. Not only had some been drafted to other ships, one party of artificers and stokers were also pressed into running trains between Singapore and Kuala Lumpar whilst another party under three sub-lieutenants were sent to Prai on Malaya's west coast to man the ferries plying between Penang Island and the main-land. The bulk of the Royal Marine survivors were formed into a fighting battalion and attached to the Argyll and Sutherland Highlanders whereby they became known as the 'Plymouth Argylls' after the football team of Plymouth, their home barracks. About half a dozen of the men who were sent to Penang were later court martialled for desertion when, after weeks of operating under constant bombing attacks, they left

89

their posts and joined a party of soldiers headed for Singapore. The sub-lieutenant in charge, now bereft of a crew, soon followed them and he, too, was court martialled even if he had entertained the idea of rounding up his crew and returning to his post. The court chose to disbelieve him and he was found guilty of desertion as were the men.

We were due to join the Exeter on Saturday, 19th of December and, on the day before, I managed to get into Singapore again. There had been another air raid the previous evening, the second night in succession and I noticed a considerable amount of damage to houses outside the city. I went straight to the France's house but only she was at home, looking apprehensive and nervous. Major France was up country and not expected back for some time so I took myself off shortly before five o'clock after a brief visit. I found a yellow taxi. The driver demanded an exorbitant fare to take me back to Johore, perhaps in confirmation of the fear infecting the local populace. We were soon out of town and while moving along the main road leading to the naval base, an Army truck suddenly swung out into our path from a side road. There was no time to stop and we collided with a shattering impact. I remembered being flung out of the car and seeing the road coming towards me and then a sudden red haziness and no more.

I regained consciousness through a haze of a drugged sleep in a light and airy hospital ward with high white walls. Soon, a nursing sister was leaning over me examining my eyes. She told me I had been unconscious when I was brought in. I had fractured my left wrist which was in plaster and had lacerations down my left side. I stared at her in disbelief as I pondered the strange quirk of fate which had allowed me to survive the trauma of the previous week only to become incapacitated in such a common-place, mundane manner. The next day a RNVR Paymaster sub-lieutenant came to see me and informed me that the Exeter had sailed. He seemed somewhat annoyed that I had missed my ship although I assured him I had similar feelings. He wanted to know how I had come to be injured as the medical authorities had merely reported my arrival at the hospital in an unconscious and injured state after finding my identity card in my top pocket. When I told him what had happened, he looked quite incredulous, his mind grappling with this quirk of fate. There seemed to be an element of tragic-comedy in a survivor of the Prince of Wales being hit by an army truck and I had to agree with him that I did feel a little absurd. After taking down more particulars from me, he left saying in a somewhat lofty tone, "God knows what we will do with you when you get out."

The hospital was located in Outram Road and, as air raids increased, more and more injured were brought in, As I was not allowed up, I was transferred to the naval Base hospital to make bed space at Outram Road. The day after Christmas, which had passed almost unnoticed except that we had a better meal and there was smuggled in Tiger beer, I was taken back to the Base by naval truck together with three ex-Repulse ratings who had been injured in an air raid. Apart from the danger of daily air raids, Outram Road had been a pleasant place and the competent, no-nonsense but compassionate demeanour of the nursing sisters did much to compensate for my disappointment. As we drove away in a downpour on the afternoon of the 26th December, none of us imagined that within about seven weeks, this hospital would be the scene of one of the most bestial and horrifying outrages perpetrated by the Japanese when they entered Singapore on the 14th of February. Only many years later we were to learn of how the Japanese soldiers sacked the hospital, systematically bayoneted all the patients, raped the nurses and indiscriminately shot members of staff.

Back at the Naval Base, there was some evidence of recent bombing but nothing like the damage which had already been caused in Singapore City. In the hospital, they put me back into bed after the Surgeon-Commander discovered that this was the second time that I had been badly concussed within seven months. I was thankful because my head seemed to ache continuously. The Sick Bay was full of recently injured officers and ratings but most of the wounded survivors had been discharged or sent home. I soon became the object of some interest when they heard how I had been injured and there was some wry comments on the competence of Army drivers and the strange quirks of fate. For the most part, we did very little except read or sleep and eat, play chess, draughts or 'uckers and listen to the news on the radio which was full of foreboding, despite the efforts of the local military command to dismiss recent British withdrawals in Malaya merely as 'strategic' or 'regrouping for counter attack.'

By the New Year, the Japanese were raiding Singapore with impunity at least twice a day. At about ten o'clock each morning, they would pass over us flying towards the city and, on their return, bomb and strafe either the Base or, more frequently, the nearby airfield of Seletar. At about three o'clock in the afternoon, they would return for a matinee performance and, taking shelter each day, became a matter of routine for us. At about this time, we heard that the Japanese were fighting south of Ipoh and had landed at Kuala Seiangor, some miles to the north of Kuala Lumpur.

I was finally discharged from the sick bay on January the 2nd and reported to the Commander's office after having searched in vain for my rather meagre possessions. Although I still had my cap, my white tropical shorts and shirts had been badly torn at the time of my accident and, when I reported to the Commander's office, I had the appearance of being in somewhat reduced circumstances. After making arrangements for me to have more kit and a promise to get me out of Singapore as soon as possible, I was given the dull task of supervising a party of recuperating seamen on 'light duties' making an inventory of stores. The seamen were, in fact, doing well without me but cheerfully accepted me realising that I, too, was only killing time. The Naval Base itself was almost empty now, both the Mauritius and the Exeter having long departed. From time to time, a destroyer would put in and we heard that a number of convoys had reached Singapore with reinforcements and supplies in the previous few days. On the 8th of January, I was sent for from the Commander's office where I was interviewed by an elderly RNVR Lieutenant-commander who, after a few solicitous questions about my health, informed me that I was to proceed to join the Exeter and should be prepared to leave for Batavia in Java the next day with a draft of seamen under a lieutenant. I was to subsequently learn however, that the Exeter arrived in Singapore on January 13th having escorted a convoy bringing the British 18th Division to Singapore and

I remain, to this day, somewhat mystified as to why I was despatched post-haste to Batavia the week before. When, some time later, I mentioned it to a senior officer, he merely said, "The Navy, like God, moves in mysterious ways."

I was quite happy to be swept up like a piece of flotsam from the Naval Base when I joined the draft for Batavia under the command of Lieutenant Habgood, a cheerful, competent New Zealander who had recently commanded an armed trawler. However, as we were about to board a lorry for the journey to Singapore, the air raid sirens sounded and, when hastening away to take cover, we saw a very large formation of six flights of nine Japanese bombers flying at about 20,000 feet directly over the causeway and heading south. The Japanese flew with a minimum of three flights of nine aircraft each up to a total of eighty-one aeroplanes in their heaviest raids. They usually dropped their bombs simultaneously on a certain signal from the leading aircraft with the most devastating effect.

After some time, the all-clear sounded and we left the Base at a good speed which was, however, soon reduced to a crawl when we reached the main road and joined heavy traffic heading southwards into the face of an army convoy moving northwards in another heavy downpour of rain.

Soon after passing an outlying village, we noticed a pall of smoke rising from Singapore and, as we inched our way into the city, the scene was hardly recognisable as the place we had known only a few weeks before. The roads were clogged with abandoned, burnt-out and smashed vehicles. Military convoys were being waved on by sweating military policemen. Lamp-posts leant over in weird, twisted shapes, shattered trees with their leaves forming a carpet beneath them lined the roads and smoke rose from burning buildings. Everywhere there were dazed people, some walking aimlessly and others standing in forlorn groups of tired, dispirited people. Wounded soldiers were standing near their vehicles and ambulances. After many detours to avoid the fires that were still raging and waiting in traffic jams at intersections, we eventually made the sea front near Raffles Hotel and turned right towards the docks. The area surrounding Collyers Quay was a complete shambles of still burning buildings, torn bomb-craters and abandoned cars and, at the harbour, there were more buildings on fire and large squads of shirtless soldiers loading equipment into lorries. After a further interminable wait in the breathless, stifling heat, we were eventually ferried out to a battered looking old transport, the Halda, lying in Singapore Roads already laden with a large draft of R.A.F. men being evacuated to Java.

During the late afternoon and just before we sailed, the air raid sirens sounded once again and, shortly afterwards, Japanese bombers, glinting in the afternoon sun, were laying yet another carpet of bombs in the densely populated area surrounding the docks. After about twenty minutes, the bombers flew off northwards and, in the rapidly fading dusk, Halda weighed and proceeded. We watched from the deck of the ship as Singapore receded into the distance with the smoke of many fires hanging as a haze in the darkening sky. While I still believed Singapore to be impregnable I was nevertheless thankful to leave the now forlorn Naval Base with its pervasive air of despondency which had prevailed since the loss of the Prince of Wales and Repulse. Not only was this a total and unique disaster, a serious blow to the pride and self esteem of the Royal Navy, it also meant the virtual disappearance of any extensive ability to dispute the Japanese on-rush through the waters of South East Asia and inevitably fore-shadowed the over-running of British possessions in the Far East. The loss of these ships and the loss of Singapore two months later, were events not only of direct and immediate values, but symbolic losses as well. Very few of us appreciated this verdict of history at that time. Our minds concentrated on our immediate problems and dangers - although I did briefly contemplate the contrast in our proud arrival and our somewhat ignominious departure just over a month later.

The next day we were off Banka Island, scene of many massacres to come when the Japanese intercepted scores of small boats and craft fleeing from Singapore during the later days of February. We crossed the equator and, during the following night, we reduced speed and hove to off Batavia where we finally berthed in the early hours of the 11th of January. The harbour was full of small to medium sized ships but there was no sign of the Exeter, nor of any other large naval units.

As I had no idea to whom I should report I remained closely attached to Habgood and his party and, when we finally disembarked, we were all taken to a green corrugated iron warehouse within the dock area, where Habgood then left us. This warehouse was full of mail-bags and there was a harassed RNVR sublieutenant in charge as mail officer. He told us to rest on a pile of these bags. I managed to ask him where the Exeter was. If anyone should have known, it should have been him as the mail officer but he did not, or would not, enlighten me. We languished in the increasing heat and torpor of this warehouse and, as the day wore on, it became unbearably hot. Finally, in the middle of the afternoon, Habgood returned in a civilian car and took me off leaving the party of fairly disgruntled ratings saying that he would be back for them shortly.

We drove to the recently established naval headquarters in an imposing building in what happened to be the main residential area where villas with white stucco walls, tiled roofs and great, shaded verandas reflected the wealth and sense of order of the Dutch colonists. This well ordered air was somewhat illusory for behind the neat, Dutch colonial façade of the naval headquarters, there were many harassed naval officers trying to cope with an increasing flow of new arrivals like myself. I finally persuaded a lugubrious looking RNVR officer to take an interest in my rather nebulous state and he said he remembered seeing a signal with my name on it. This was followed by about five minutes of searching through files on his desk, into drawers and a battered looking filing cabinet until he finally unearthed a piece of paper, waving it into the air with grunts of achievement. He studied it intently with frequent indecisive interjections, the odd sigh and cough, all confirming that he really did not know what to do with me. He spoke to someone on the phone and finally said I was to remain in Batavia until the Exeter returned and, in the meantime, I would be given a job in one of the outlying sub-offices of the embryo naval headquarters.

Batavia was hotter and more humid than Singapore lying supinely on the flattest and most uninteresting part of the coast of Java and at the foot of the cool uplands of Bandoeng. From its beginnings in the early 17th century as a fortified warehouse near the original village of Dayakarta, the Dutch established a completely new city of intersecting canals, small houses with narrow windows and burnt red-tiled roofs as a tropical replica of Amsterdam. Soon, however, this once healthy sea-port became one of the pestholes of the world and for centuries was known as the grave-yard of the Orient when its network of canals turned out to be the ideal breeding ground for malarial mosquitoes. In October 1770, Captain Cook put in here in HMS Endeavour to effect repairs at the dock-yard at Pulau Onrust, where his tireless and intelligent attention to the health of his crew during the two years of his voyage was undone when malaria and dysentery brought death to many of his men. While the Dutch had long since moved out of the old city into splendid residential areas, the old city of Kota remained as it had for a hundred years – a rundown, decayed, hectic city of stinking canals, potholes and broken pavements.

The next few weeks had a suspended quality about them. I was billeted in a tented dormitory set up in the grounds of a substantial house which served as the wardroom and, every day, I went to work in a very hot and stuffy little room at the naval office, correcting confidential books from a vast pile of amendment pages. It was my task to wade through these with scissors, pen and glue bringing them up to date. And, in the evenings, I would retire to the nearby swimming club with a number of congenial companions and follow it with a gigantic Javanese dinner of hot delicacies and rice washed down with excellent Amstel beer. On one occasion, we went to a sumptuous lunch at Hotel des Indes. I was also financially well off as I had been given a number of advances of pay which, when I came to work it out, I discovered, I was two months ahead of the navy. This period was by way of being a respite for me and I gradually felt my self confidence and alertness returning after weeks of lethargy, confused thinking and disappointments. I also enjoyed a certain standing amongst my betters as a survivor of the Prince of Wales and

96

I admit to unscrupulously trading upon it at times with my still-plastered wrist adding unspoken testimony when I neglected to say precisely how it had come to be broken.

But, as each day passed, our rather carefree attitudes were replaced by increasing apprehension as we learned of further Japanese successes and Allied failures. The Philippines had been overrun early in the New Year, landing in Borneo and the Celebes, and now the Japanese were within thirty miles of Singapore. As we discussed these events amongst ourselves, it was plain that the Japanese were driving a vast pincer movement towards Java and if Singapore was to be invested and by-passed with a simultaneous thrust from Borneo, we would soon be defending Java. But there had been cheering news for us for we knew of additional troops arriving in Java and of consignments of new Hurricane fighters to reinforce the RAF who were now building up their strength at airfields near Batavia and Soerabaya. The local Dutch population seemed serene and confident that Java would be held although I did not come into much contact with them except for those I saw in the various shops and in the street.

On the 10th of February, we heard that the Japanese had crossed the Johore Causeway and had gained a foothold in Singapore. I was stunned at this news and found it incomprehensible that it was only two months since they had opened their assault upon us and the Prince of Wales and Repulse had been lost. On the same day, I was told that the Exeter would arrive in Batavia the next morning.

I joined ship at 9 o'clock on the 11th of February and reported to the officer-in-charge of midshipmen who introduced me to the Commander, Commander Richardson, and later to the Captain, Captain Gordon.

The Exeter was of 8,390 tons displacement, 575 feet in length with a maximum speed of 32 knots and was armed with six 8 inch, four 4 inch and six 21 inch torpedo tubes and carried a crew of 700 officers and ratings.

The Exeter and her sister ship the York, which was now a rusting hulk in Suda Bay, Crete, were the only two ships of a class of eight-inch gun cruisers built in accordance with pre-war restrictions of the

Washington Conference whereby her main armament had been reduced from eight to six 8 inch guns. Furthermore, Exeter's cruising range was restricted to 10,000 miles at economical speed (14 knots) which was well below the range of the 8 inch gun County class cruisers built for long range cruising and protection of shipping routes. As a result, both the Exeter and the York had become something of a joke in pre-war naval circles of which the most charitable was that they had been designed for sale to a potential enemy. Nevertheless, the Exeter was, at this time, one of the more famous ships of the Royal Navy having borne the brunt of the action which led to the scuttling of the German pocket-battleship, the Graf Spee, after the Battle of the River Plate in 1939. Now on a new commission, she had been escorting a convoy in the Bay of Bengal when the Japanese declared war from whence she was despatched post haste to Singapore, arriving on that fateful day that the Prince of Wales and the Repulse was sunk. Since then she had been almost continuously engaged on convoy escort and protection duties through the Sunda Straits to Singapore bringing in reinforcements, her weather beaten appearance and tired crew betraying many days and nights at sea.

I found my former companions in the gunroom including Errington who was in his usual high spirits.

"What was she like?" he asked and, when I looked blank, he said, "Come on, you don't expect us to believe that cock and bull story about being hit by an army lorry, do you? We had it on good authority that you had got your feet under the table of a Chinese bint and you were wounded in action," and much more in the same vein. It was good to be back amongst them.

By some devious and mysterious way, my journal which I had been handed at the Naval Base at Singapore upon departure for onward transmission, arrived on board the same day with other confidential documents. This was my new journal with my account of the sinking of the Prince of Wales but before it had been read by Snotty Nurse who had merely pencilled in the margin, "Your journal is well written up."

For the next two days, the Exeter refuelled and stored from a store ship in the harbour. During this time, there were continuous arrivals of other naval units. The Dutch cruisers, De Ruyter, Java and Tromp, all with 5.9 inch main armament entered harbour with four destroyers although the Tromp looked to us to be neither cruiser nor destroyer but modelled on the lines of the very large German fleet destroyers. Later a flotilla of six American destroyers entered harbour and anchored and, finally, the Australian cruiser, Hobart, arrived with the Danae which we had last seen in Singapore. Clearly such a concentration of ships presaged an operation of some significance even if it was a motley collection of stained and sea weary ships. With the exception of the Dutch cruiser, Tromp, all ships were old and weakly armed, particularly with anti-aircraft armament. The Dutch cruiser Java looked to be of vintage proportions and the American destroyers all had narrow, top-heavy lines. But perhaps our most serious weakness which would manifest itself in a particularly disastrous manner was the lack of a common doctrine between the captains of three different navies when attempting to act in concert.

At 18.00 hours on February 14th 1942, the Exeter, in company with the de Ruyter, flying the flag of Rear Admiral Doorman of the Royal Netherland Navy, Java, Tromp, Hobart, four Dutch and six U.S. destroyers weighed and proceeded from Batavia. Once clear of the harbour, we formed a line ahead with a screen of destroyers on a nor'- nor'- westerly course at a speed of 22 knots.

On leaving harbour, hands closed up to action stations. We were told that a large Japanese convoy had been sighted to the west of Anamba Island and thought to be headed for Banka Island and the Palembang area of Sumatra. It was the intention to disrupt this landing by attacking the convoy early next day. The similarity of this intention with that which followed our departure from Singapore in the Prince of Wales only two months ago did not go entirely unnoticed by myself, particularly as we had, once again, no air cover. We remained at defence stations and preparations for action were immediately put in hand. Throughout the night, the force steamed northwards and, during the early hours of the morning watch, passed through the Gasper Straits between Banka and Billiton Islands in the South China Sea. Hands closed up to dawn action just before the first streaks of unpremeditated dawn began to lighten the sky on the east. Sunrise followed shortly after and it was soon hot with a brilliant sea and a hard blue sky.

14ᵗʰ February 1942. HMS Exeter in action against Japanese aircraft in the South China Sea

At about an hour after sunrise, de Ruyter reported an aircraft on the northern horizon and soon we could see what appeared to be a seaplane pursuing its customary shadowing tactics, soon disappearing into the morning's haze. Immediately 'Repel aircraft station' was sounded and we hastened to our action stations. Once again I felt some uneasiness and, with an assurance born of recent experience, I informed the signalman standing next to me, "They'll soon be here." He seemed unimpressed having apparently seen shadowing aircraft for weeks without any dire consequences. Feeling somewhat like a Jonah, my prediction was soon however to be filled for there were now reports of 'ten plus bogeys' approaching from the north east and, low on the horizon, we saw a group of fast approaching aircraft. As with the second attack on the Prince of Wales, these split into two separate flights and flew around the horizon out of range but, instead of losing height, began to gain height on our beam in readiness for high speed dive bombing attacks which developed shortly.

As we began to take avoiding action, we could hear the whine of aircraft rising to a crescendo above the crack of our 4 inch guns which were engaging and within seconds a line of bombs exploded in the sea some distance away on our starboard side. As we emerged from behind the falling founts of the bomb bursts, I saw one of the American destroyers almost leap from the sea as two near misses straddled her. By this time, there were anti aircraft bursts all over the sky and it appeared that each ship was being attacked simultaneously by groups of two or three aircraft. Within about five minutes, the attacking aircraft had disappeared and it occurred to me that, as on previous occasions, one rarely noticed attacking aircraft breaking off. One minute they were there and then they were gone. This was perhaps merely a reflex reaction as one immediately began to look inward to one's own ship to assess what damage had been done. In our case, there was none, all bombs having fallen wide but two American destroyers were seen to drop astern and alter course southwards as a result of damage by near misses.

The squadron then reformed in line ahead and we continued our northerly course and, within ten minutes, there were, once again, reports of aircraft in the immediate vicinity. Suddenly, from astern of us, Hobart began engaging a flight of about six low flying aircraft approaching from the south. These were obviously carrier borne aircraft, small and fast and each carrying a single bomb. Soon they peeled off in all directions and one of these approached Exeter fine on the starboards quarter and was engaged by the after 4 inch armament and close range weapons. At the last moment however, the Japanese pilot changed his mind and swerved away boring towards the Tromp just ahead of us. But he was obviously unnerved because he dropped his bomb into the sea between the two of us.

Within twenty minutes, a third attack developed from high level bombers and, for the next hour, we took avoiding action from successive waves of bombers. Incredibly, no one was hit. After this attack and with no obvious damage to any of the cruiser squadron, I began to feel somewhat more confident than I had when we had first sighted the shadower, fearing a repetition of the events of only eight weeks ago. Within ten minutes of the Japanese breaking off their last attack, the Admiral signalled a reversal of course and an increase of speed to 25 knots. We remained closed up at action stations for the remainder of the morning as the squadron now steamed back through the Gasper Strait towards Java. The Captain addressed the crew over the ship's address system and said that the squadron was withdrawing southwards in the face of clear evidence of the presence of a Japanese carrier force within the vicinity to which we, without air cover, would be extremely vulnerable. I, for one, saw the wisdom of this.

At about 9 pm, Exeter and Hobart parted company with the Dutch and American ships altering course to pass through the Sunda Strait while we proceeded directly to Batavia where we arrived after midnight and anchored. Early the next morning, we heard that Singapore had surrendered the previous day and our sortie had not prevented the Japanese from landing in Sumatra. Later that day, we also heard that Bali, to the east of Java, had been captured by the Japanese and that the Japanese had bombed Darwin in Australia. Above all, it was the news of the surrender of Singapore that stunned us. At that moment we felt neither disgrace nor humiliation but merely concern for the many people that we knew and perhaps left behind in Singapore. I wondered what had become of the Frances. Had they managed to get away or had they been trapped? Perhaps we all vaguely felt that things would never be the same again and so it proved to be for the fall of Singapore was to become one of the major milestones of history, a precursor to the eclipse of an entire Empire. Many have since analysed the reasons, many thousands of words written on final, personal agonies and all of us are only too aware of the horrors inflicted on many thousands of people by the conquering Japanese. A third of a century later, the debacle was finally and succinctly best summarised by that eloquent observer of Empire, Jan Morris who wrote;

The convictions of two centuries were knocked topsy-turvy by this event and Asians were never to look on Englishmen in quite the same way again. The Royal Navy had failed; the British armies had been outclassed; white men had been seen in states of panic and humility; the legend had collapsed in pathos – or worse still, bathos for the Generals were second rate, the songs were banal, the policies were ineffective and even the courage was less than universal.

Throughout that hot, stifling day, we remained in harbour expecting to hear that the British forces had somehow thrown the Japanese back out of Singapore but, sadly, as the day wore on, such fanciful optimism was replaced with the awful truth that Singapore had gone the way of Hong Kong and Manila in some terrible whirlwind of unalloyed misfortune. There were no doubts in our minds that Java was now the next objective, the richest prize of the Indies and, for the first time since the Japanese war began, I started to feel demoralised by a creeping helplessness. The Japanese had already taken Bali and had landed in southern Sumatra thus effectively blocking the only exits through the Sunda, Bali or Lombok Straits to the Indian Ocean. The way to the east was also barred by the Japanese landings in Borneo and the Celebes. We now also heard rumours, later substantiated, of an engagement fought at the beginning of the month between Japanese Naval forces and a mixed Dutch/American force in the Macassar Straits where the American cruisers, Houston and Marblehead had been badly damaged. Nothing we could do seemed to stem the Japanese onrush and there were many of us who felt we should immediately withdraw from the area while there was still time. But, somehow, we knew we would have to remain. There were over 100,000 Europeans in Java alone and there were reports of a vast armada of ships and small craft fleeing Singapore, heavily laden with refugees and making for Java.

The next day, the 17th of February, I was sent to the naval headquarters ashore to bring back confidential documents. While I was at the jetty, a small ship arrived carrying refugees from

Singapore. They were mostly British citizens, men, women and some small children and they all had a dazed, remote look about them. This was the first to arrive for there were many more ship loads and they seemed to cause considerable concern and consternation ashore. I met Charles Younger, one of my erstwhile companions of a few weeks ago at naval headquarters. He had apparently been charged with certain aspects of their reception, seeing them moved on to Australia if possible. He was harassed and depressed by what he had heard about the Japanese behaviour in Malaya but even more so by instances of monstrous behaviour from those whom he would have expected better. That morning he had been involved in removing and arresting a group of Australian soldiers from a recently arrived ship in response to the captain who reported that, before leaving Singapore, they had forced their way on board at bayonet point and demanded to be evacuated. Courage did seem to be less than universal.

Another Australian cruiser arrived at Tanjong Prick on the 19th of February, HMAS Perth together with the destroyers Jupiter, Electra and Encounter. I was pleased to see the Electra again, one of the Prince of Wales faithful watch dogs and a ship I somehow felt a special bond with. She had been with us during the Bismarck operation and had picked up the only three survivors from the Hood and had been with us on our long voyage east, during our final moments of Kuantan and had finally brought the Repulse's survivors back to Singapore. I had last seen the Jupiter and Encounter in Singapore after they had accompanied us from Colombo on our voyage out and we soon learned of the Jupiter's notable success in having already sunk a Japanese submarine a few weeks ago in the Sunda Strait – a bright, brief flash of success in an otherwise calamitous month by a ship well known throughout the fleet as a 'notorious crock.'

At about this time, we heard that the Allied naval forces were to be split into two main groups, a British/ Australian squadron to be based at Batavia and a Dutch/American squadron on Soerabaya to counter the Japanese threat to Java on its western and eastern flanks respectively. The British/Australian squadron would consist of the Exeter, Hobart, Perth, Danae, Dragon and the three destroyers.

We remained in Tanjong Prick during the following days carrying out urgent maintenance work after the many hard days of steaming that Exeter had been subject to over the previous two months. It also enabled us to get ashore for brief periods. Bratavia had changed dramatically in the last few days. There were more and more British servicemen and, one afternoon, we were treated to the reassuring sight of a flight of six Hurricane fighters flying over the city. This well-ordered city with its solid citizens suddenly seemed to spring to life in a fit of confused apprehension as more and more refugees arrived from Singapore with dismal tales of incompetence and bungling and of Japanese atrocities so bizarre and incomprehensible that we tended to discount many as fabrications justifying their precipitate flight. We were soon to discover the truth of many of these tales but so were we to learn, many years later, of many more shameful and discreditable episodes which marred other accounts of self sacrifice during the final days of Singapore. Perhaps it was just as well that we knew nothing of these at the time because, despite everything, we somehow optimistically believed we would, in the end, halt the Japanese onrush. I remember gazing across the anchorage at the line of ships, their white ensigns only faintly disturbed in the gentle breeze, boats travelling to and fro with a purposeful bustle and thinking that we presented a formidable force. My own experience, however, should have told me that without the vital element of air superiority, these weakly armed and tired ships really had little chance against the Japanese. But it did not. My young mind was already thoroughly indoctrinated by the spirit of the Royal Navy, stubbornly convinced of our innate superiority and victim of traditions firmly rooted in the last century. We all believed in Admiral Lord St. Vincent when he said, "I do not say the French cannot come, I only say they cannot come by sea." It somehow did not seem to have entered our consciousness that this legendary example of the Navy's ruthless absolutism had already been superseded by the invention of the aeroplane half a century ago.

105

On the 25th of February at 16.00 hours the Exeter and Perth with the destroyers Jupiter, Electra and Encounter weighed anchor and proceeded. Once clear of the harbour, the force turned eastward and increased speed to 22 knots. Throughout the night and following morning, we proceeded eastward along the northern coast of Java towards Soerabaya. We remained at defence stations throughout but, apart from the odd sightings of two Dutch reconnaissance sea-planes and a number of small native craft, the sky remained clear and hot. Shortly after noon, we arrived off the minefields guarding the entrance to Soerabaya and, after threading our way through a swept channel, anchored off the basin at 4p.m. Here we found the Dutch flagship, de Ruyter, with its heavy, odd-shaped superstructure, the cruiser Java, the USS Houston and a mixed flotilla of seven Dutch and American destroyers all obviously making preparations for sea. We remained ready for sea with steam at all engines whilst the destroyers refuelled inside the dock basin and the Captain went ashore. He returned about sunset and, shortly afterwards, the ship prepared to sail on a night still hot and heavy with an air of urgency dispelling the enervating torpor.

We weighed and proceeded at 19.00 hours on the 26th in company with de Ruyter flying the flag of the Dutch Rear Admiral Doorman, Houston, Berth, Java and ten British, Dutch and American destroyers. Upon clearing the narrow channel through the minefield, the squadron set course eastwards until, late that night, the course was reversed to the west.

We were told that we had sailed in response to reports of a large Japanese invasion convoy force moving southward some 200 miles to the north-eastwards and we could expect to be in action during the early hours of the next morning. We remained at action stations throughout the night with a few of us being allowed to sleep at our quarters. I could not sleep. I was overcome with a rising excitement at the prospect of action and spent my time scanning the horizon in the light of a nearly full moon. Just before first light, we stood at quarters but, as the pale light rapidly brightened into another hot, glassy day, the horizon remained clear but only for a moment. Soon after sunrise, two aircraft were sighted low down on the horizon pursuing their now familiar shadowing tactics. After some time, they disappeared but, from about 9.30 onwards, a series of single Japanese aircraft flew over the squadron dropping a few bombs in an off-hand manner, quite uncharacteristic of what we had come to expect from them. Soon afterwards they, too, disappeared to the northward and, at about 10.30 when the force was some 60 miles to the north of Soerabaya, our course was reversed for a return to port. For many of us, this manoeuvre was puzzling for it smacked of a lack of purpose after the expectations generated by our urgent and purposeful departure from Soerabaya the previous evening.

Land was sighted early in the afternoon but, as the squadron was preparing to enter the swept channel leading to the harbour, there was a sudden flurry of signals ordering a reversal of course and an increase in speed. Once again we were called back to action stations, the urgent bugle notes now dispelling the anti-climax of the last few hours. We soon learned that the invasion convoy that we had searched vainly for all that morning had now been sighted some 90 miles to the north of Soerabaya.

Speed was increased to 20 knots as we steamed in line ahead with de Ruyter leading and the Dutch and British destroyers scouting ahead at about five miles.

Soon after 4p.m. Electra reported, 'enemy in sight,' to the north east and, within minutes, our main director and armament were training in the same direction as the ship now vibrated under the increased engine revolutions when speed was increased to about 27 knots. Soon we spotted wisps of smoke on the horizon which had coalesced into a slight discolouration of the otherwise clear blue sky on the starboard bow. Low down on the horizon, we could just make out the superstructures of what appeared to be a large squadron of warships, their masts dancing in the heat haze of the horizon. Soon the enemy squadron was identified as two four-funnelled Sendal class cruisers, each leading a division of seven Asashio class destroyers, and they were steering west-sou-west across our bows.

For the next ten minutes I could hear my own heart beats against a background of humming ventilators, the muted roar from our funnels and the sound of our urgent wake breaking the calm sea. The

107

spell was suddenly broken by a ripple of orange flashes low down on the horizon when the leading enemy cruiser opened fire on the Electra, the starboard wing destroyer of the screen. The range was then about 27,000 yards and, in reply, we opened fire on the cruiser almost immediately with our forward main armament. The range was, as yet, too great for the guns of De Ruyter and the remaining six inch gun cruisers but, before we could close on the enemy, Admiral Doorman ordered a turn to port. I was immediately struck by the similarity of our approach to that of the Hood and Prince of Wales to Bismarck ten months ago but, this time, the Dutch Admiral had correctly altered course to prevent the enemy from crossing our 'tee' thus enabling all our guns to bear. However, when the turn was ordered, the range was still too extreme for the remaining cruisers to engage and, as we steamed westward on a parallel course, the battle turned into a duel between the Exeter and Houston and the Japanese force.

Soon our salvoes were straddling the enemy cruisers but theirs were erratic with poor ranging, many salvoes falling short. After about twelve salvoes, the leading enemy cruiser turned away under smoke. Fire was then shifted to the second cruiser and, after a further ten salvoes had been fired she, too, was seen to reverse her course under smoke, belching forth a trail of thick brownish-black smoke which we all took to be a hit. This was more to our liking and we all felt cheered.

Our elation was, however, short lived, for about this time, two more cruisers, each leading a division of destroyers were sighted to the north-east following in the wake of the two, four funnelled cruisers. These new arrivals appeared to be of a larger, more modern Ashigra class. Exeter immediately shifted target to the second of these, Houston, just astern of us, having already engaged the leading cruiser. Soon ripples of fire could be seen from all the enemy cruisers as they retaliated and it became evident that we were the main target when we heard the familiar 'whoofing' sound of an approaching salvo. Our shooting remained undeterred and we were now straddling with effect followed by unmistakable signs that we had scored a hit just below the main super-structure on the second of the cruisers. A few minutes after this, we ourselves were closely straddled. A fount of water from a near miss seemed to lift the ship out of the sea. The ship gave a jarring shudder followed immediately by a deep seated explosion amidships. We had been hit.

A few seconds later, we were drawing out of line to port accompanied by a deafening roar of escaping steam and thick black smoke. We had been hit in a boiler room and even as we turned we could feel speed fall off. At that moment there seemed to be complete confusion as the ships in line astern of us all turned away. Then there were two destroyers expertly laying a smoke screen between us and the enemy. After turning away, our forward main armament recommenced firing. This time the target was one of the remaining four funnelled cruisers now leading a convoy of destroyers in a torpedo attack. With the smoke screen that the destroyers had laid down, it was difficult to understand what was happening. Everywhere there was smoke from our own guns, roaring steam and smoke from our boiler room and waves of distant gunfire and explosions reverberating across the sea. All seemed to have degenerated into a confused battle. No longer aware of what was happening, I began to feel a real fear, learning, for the first time, that in battle, knowledge tends to hold fear at bay.

Our speed had been drastically reduced to barely fourteen knots as a result of that one hit. We now turned southwards and limped out of the battle. The De Ruyter had also turned off on to a reciprocal course and soon she was overhauling us with her accompanying cruisers forming up astern and heading eastwards. As we began to fall astern, a single, modern Japanese cruiser was seen closing up on us rapidly from the northward and fine on the port quarter. Fire was immediately opened with our main after turret and the ship swung round to port to bring our forward guns to bear. This produced the desired effect for, after a few salvoes, the enemy cruiser turned away leaving a trail of smoke. It was now about 6.30.p.m. and, in the rapidly darkening tropical night, the Exeter, with an escort of a Dutch destroyer, set course for Soerabaya some sixty miles to the south eastward where, after passing through the minefield, we anchored shortly before midnight. The city was partially blacked out, comfortless and sinister with only the light of fires from earlier air raids and flares from native fishing boats lighting up the sombre, darkened land.

All of us were over-tired but the excitements of the day worked to keep some of us wide awake. A few of us gathered in the gunroom to discuss events, speculating on the outcome of the battle which had obviously continued after we had been forced to withdraw. We all felt that, although the Dutch Admiral had made the correct tactical decision by turning to port to allow all our guns to bear and thus preventing the enemy from 'crossing our tee', he had turned too soon. This had prevented the De Ruyter and the 6 inch gun cruisers from bringing their guns into action at a stage when such a move might have been decisive. Contrary to the Royal Navy's doctrine of fighting close actions, epitomised by Nelson's last signal at Trafalgar, to 'Engage the enemy more closely', the Dutch Admiral had been hesitant and obviously reluctant to fight an action at close quarters, thus forcing a battle at extreme range in which only the Exeter and the Houston were able to participate. But, perhaps the most galling to all of us was that, for the first time, the Royal Navy had been subordinated to a foreign Admiral who, although clearly not lacking in initiative, could not have had personal experience with ships and crews (with the exception of Perth) completely untried in battle.

As we discussed these finer points of tactics, we were overshadowed with a sense of foreboding and began to wonder whether we would have to fight our way out of the harbour to prevent being trapped with the unthinkable options of fighting to the finish, scuttling the ship or even capture. We knew, however, that only the first option was open to us. No British captain would ever scuttle his ship without a fight and no British warship had been captured by the enemy since Napoleonic times. The BBC news that the Allied Command in Java had been withdrawn to India only increased our doubts. From the euphemistic phrases, we gleaned that now virtually all of the Dutch East Indies were now in Japanese hands. I began to fear the dawn as we turned in that night, a real chilling fear with a gripping tension in the stomach and a fluttering contraction of the sphincter.

Shortly after dawn, the Exeter weighed anchor and proceeded to berth alongside the Dutch naval base where work was immediately started on repairing the damage. The eight inch shell had struck the starboard after 4 inch gun mounting passing through the shield, killing four of the gun crew then going on to penetrate the boat deck and on down into B boiler room. The shell did not detonate on impact but exploded in the boiler room killing ten of the men stationed there. The port pom-pom had also been damaged by a shell which appeared to have ricocheted off the after funnel.

That day proved to be a long, hot, eventful one. Work on repairing the damage went on without respite. Everyone showed signs of strain and tiredness after thirty-six hours of constant alert and battle against a background of continued bombing attacks on Soerabaya city by enemy aircraft which seemed to go on all day. Despite these frequent alarms, time was found to conduct the funeral for the fourteen men who had lost their lives the previous day in a sombre ceremony just as the sun began to set over the land to the west. During the day, the Encounter entered the anchorage and within a short time, disquieting news had spread that both the Electra and Jupiter and one Dutch destroyer had all been lost with the fate of the remainder of the squadron still in doubt. Later that day, a buzz spread through the ship that the De Ruyter and Java had also been sunk and only Houston and Perth had escaped annihilation, by withdrawing to Batavia. I subsequently found all this to be true when, years later, I discovered that even though they had escaped that night, they themselves were sunk in a valiant attempt to gain the Indian Ocean through the Sunda Strait within a day or two.

Soon after sunset, preparations were made for sea. The engineers, artificers, shipwrights and stokers had worked tirelessly in restoring steam in two of the eight boilers. The captain addressed the crew and thanked everyone for their hard work and devotion throughout the last few months and, without wishing to minimise the dangers we now faced, he felt sure we would be enabled to break out and regain the safety of the Indian Ocean. We learned that Exeter with Encounter, USS Pope and a Dutch destroyer would sail within hours for the Sunda Strait. The news was received with stoic optimism by the ship's company even though it meant running a possible gauntlet along the full length of the northern coast of Java, a distance of over 400 nautical miles. It was to be a bold but forlorn attempt.

Shortly after nightfall on Friday, February 28th, Exeter, Encounter and USS Pope proceeded out of Sourabaya through the northern channel. The Dutch destroyer stayed in the harbour. On clearing the minefield, course was set to the north-east and, at about midnight, altered to the north to pass to the eastward of Bawean Island. At about this time, two additional boilers were connected and speed was increased in stages to about 23 knots. We remained at defence stations throughout the night while the ship was secured and stripped for action. There was no protective darkness for there was now a full moon and, as the ship sailed steadily northwards through a slight sea, the moonlight seemed to grow steadily brighter and more revealing with each passing minute. I went on watch at midnight and, fighting my tiredness, busied myself with writing up the log and answering the phones. Nobody spoke and only the muted roar of the ventilator and exhaust fans and the nearby halyard rattling against the superstructure with a ticking sound as well as the sigh of the sea disturbed the general hush and quiet passing of helm orders. Shortly before the turn of the watch at 4 a.m. however, this quietness was broken by an urgent report from a port lookout, "Ships in sight, bearing red eight-oh."

In the light of the setting moon, those of us on watch could see the small, dark outline of Bawean Island and, slightly to the right, the silhouettes of three large ships heading in a southerly direction. I fully expected that we would head straight for the ships and take them by surprise and I was somewhat puzzled as the helm orders were quickly given to swing to starboard and head away towards the darker eastern horizon stern on to the enemy. After a few minutes reflection, I realised we were in no fair state to fight a night action and were probably under orders to evade rather than engage the enemy who now appeared to be passing to the westward of Bawean

Island and were soon moving out of sight. We thereupon altered course in stages to the northward again and, shortly before dawn, course was altered to the west as we closed up to action stations.

The dawn came suddenly, the sun a burning ball of fire and soon the horizon was etched deeply against the light morning sky. It was another hot, clear, beautiful day and while there was a general lessening of tension throughout the ship, we were not allowed to leave our action stations. Breakfast was brought to us, hot 'tiddley oggies' and strong tea. As I stood sipping my tea from a mug and staring out on the starboard side, I began to think that the omens were good until a signalman standing nearby said, "It's always bad luck to sail on a Friday."

And so it eventually proved to be for, at about 7. 50 am, the crow's nest lookout reported the masts of two ships almost dead ahead, steering to the north-east and diagonally across our bows. Exeter immediately reversed course and headed directly into the sun which, it was thought, would blind the Japanese lookouts. But this was not to be for we noticed that they had already turned towards us. We had been spotted. But once again reprieve seemed to be at hand when, after a few minutes, the enemy cruisers returned to their original course of north-east and were soon lost from sight. After a short interval, course was altered in stages to the southward and eventually back to our original westerly course. Once again our spirits began to rise for it seemed that luck was indeed again with us on this voyage and for the next hour and a half, Exeter continued her westward course while everyone at action stations on deck strained their eyes to the horizon, the tension waning with each passing minute.

These gradually rising expectations were however soon shattered when, about 9.30 am, the top-masts of two heavy cruisers were sighted to the southward and steering a parallel westerly course, Once again Exeter immediately turned away to the northwards but it was clear that we had been spotted because they too turned towards us and this time they kept coming. All eyes were strained astern as a chase now seemed to be developing although we all knew that we could not out-distance our pursuers with steam in only half our boilers. Then, suddenly a report came of an enemy ship heading directly towards us from dead ahead.

This was soon identified as an enemy destroyer and, at 20,000 yards, we opened fire with the main armament. Both Encounter and Pope, some 5,000 yards ahead on the screen opened fire on the destroyer and, after a few minutes, it turned away under smoke. Almost simultaneously, two more large cruisers were sighted to the northward and these, at once, turned towards us. We appeared to have sailed into a trap which was now about to be sprung.

We altered course 90 degrees to the east with the destroyers following around, in a further effort to evade the enemy force which had now been identified as four Asahigara or Atago class cruisers all armed with ten 8 inch guns. It took me some time to realise how formidable a force the enemy had now ranged against us and were obviously intent on closing in from both sides. It did not need any feat of premonition to foretell that it would only be a matter of time before we would be sunk. Somehow, the sea held no terrors for me but the uncertainty of what would happen once the enemy ships found their range filled me with a moment of terror manifested by a sharp, gripping pain in the bowels, with my tongue sticking to the roof of my suddenly very dry mouth.

Both enemy cruisers were now roughly following parallel courses at about 25,000 yards, the southern pair on our starboard beam and the northern pair on our port quarter. At this extreme range the leading northern cruiser opened fire and Exeter immediately replied but our salvoes fell wide of the target in contrast to our accurate shooting of two days previously. This, I learned later, was because of a fault in the fire control table which was only discovered after a number of salvoes had been fired.

After the enemy cruiser had found the range, Pope and Encounter began laying a heavy smoke screen which effectively screened us from either side and our own responses became intermittent whenever a target appeared through the smoke. At the same time, the ship was taking evasive action by snaking a course to avoid straddles and steering from the enemy shell splashes. As the ship heeled over in response to these frequent alterations of course, the horizon was now obscured by smoke and a familiar wailing whoofing sound filled the air as successive enemy salvoes fell around us. Incredibly this went on for the next ninety minutes without any damage to ourselves and I began to feel optimistic once again as the enemy cruisers seemed reluctant to close the range. Although it was my duty to keep an accurate log of events, I found it difficult as there was a moment when we simultaneously fired torpedoes from the port tubes at the northern group of cruisers, the 4 inch secondary armament opened fire on a group of enemy destroyers which had since appeared on the starboard side and then again at two spotting aircraft as we were altering course to open the arcs of our forward armament. We were now fighting back with everything including dropping smoke floats over the stern and, for a few moments, I was exhilarated.

Despite this momentary return of confidence, the situation at about 11 o'clock was nevertheless ominous. Main armament ammunition was reported to be getting low and, despite a superhuman effort on the part of the engine room in connecting one further boiler, we were still only able to steam at about 25 knots. But our luck continued to hold. We still had not been seriously damaged and the two divisions of enemy cruisers were still reluctant to close the action. But finally and inevitably, after nearly two hours of holding off, a far superior enemy in a running fight, Exeter was hit in a boiler room.

There was a heavy explosion amidships. Smoke and fumes shrouded the ship as a fierce fire started. Shortly afterwards, the whole ship shuddered as further enemy shells crashed into the after superstructure and hull and reports of a fire aft were now reaching the bridge. Within minutes our speed began to fall off as steam pressure dropped with all power failing shortly afterwards, which meant that the main armament could no longer be trained nor elevated. As we slowed, Encounter and Pope drew ahead and the enemy fire became highly effective with frequent straddles and hits being obtained amidships. The whole ship was now shrouded in a pall of smoke and unable to retaliate. The end was suddenly and swiftly upon us. The order to 'sink the ship' was passed and, shortly afterwards, 'Abandon ship'.

We immediately cleared the compass platform and I made my way as fast as I could to the focsle deck where a group of men were throwing floats, flot-a-nets and woodwork into the sea. By this time the ship had a decided list to port but was still moving through the water at about 4 knots. While groups of men were jumping into the sea and others were letting themselves down by ropes, I was, for the second time in my short naval career, frozen into immobility. While the sea was, on this occasion, comfortably nearer than when we had abandoned the Prince of Wales, the prospect of being sucked under the wake of a moving ship seemed that much more perilous. It was only when I heard a man standing near me shout, "Christ, we'll all be killed in the water. They're still firing at us," that I was illogically galvanised into action and, in a sudden movement of abandonment, I jumped. Fortunately I fell clear but there were shell and splinter splashes all around us, oil on the water and a short, sharp chop to the sea caused by the ship's wake and a slight breeze. When I stopped swimming, I noticed that the ship was already receding from us but enemy shells were still straddling and hitting her. Then, as we watched from the sea, there came a tremendous explosion followed by a hammer-blow shock wave passing through the water and which seemed to hold my body in a vice like grip. Towering well above the superstructure was a fount of water and it was clear that the Exeter had been delivered a coup de grace by an enemy torpedo. The ship then righted itself and, for a moment, it remained upright, shrouded in smoke, her ensigns still flying before she began settling to starboard and then, more quickly with an accelerating roll, she slid upside down beneath the waves. In contrast to the lack of emotion that I had felt when I watched the Prince of Wales slide beneath the waves, I was overcome with a strong sense of loss. The Exeter was a ship of character with hard earned battle honours from the River Plate in 1939, Britain's first naval victory of the war and there were not many people in Britain who had not heard her name. She had acquitted herself with honour in her final battle by fighting to the last against vastly superior forces – her six eight inch guns against a combined total of forty eight inch guns of the four Japanese cruisers for more than two hours.

The sea was now strewn with wreckage, floats and men and the Japanese had ceased firing. Seeing a float with about twenty men clinging to it, I slowly swam towards it and was hauled aboard, which is how I came to be barely afloat in the sea on a hot, bright, Sunday afternoon some miles to the north of Java with England many thousands of miles away.

Last moments of HMS Exeter sunk by Japanese Cruisers and Destroyers in the Java sea 1ˢᵗ March 1942.
(Photo taken by observer in Japanese aircraft)

****

We re-entered Soerabaya harbour on board a Japanese destroyer on 3rd of March only three days after we had sailed in the Exeter in a bold but futile attempt to break through the Sunda Strait to regain the Indian Ocean. The harbour was now crowded with Japanese troop transports and naval escort vessels. It was almost as if we had gone out of one door and the Japanese had entered by the other. Maybe it was just as well that we had sailed when we did otherwise we might have well been caught at the anchorage. After a long wait outside the inner harbour, we eventually berthed alongside at dusk and it wasn't long before we were herded ashore where our fortunes took a turn for the worse when we suddenly found ourselves in the hands of the Japanese army.

We were told to leave the four seriously injured men on board and the rest of us were ordered ashore. We filed down the narrow gangway to be greeted by blows from an ugly group of soldiers on the quay. These were not just taps but good hard blows to the ribs and head with rifle butts and some of us were slashed with bayonets.

The Japanese sailors looked on impassively from the decks of the destroyers as we were formed into a semblance of a line, while an N.C.O. strutted in front of us haranguing us in Japanese which, although not understanding a word, was unmistakenly a series of bellicose threats. There were five soldiers, all armed with rifles and long, ugly looking bayonets, who looked to be tough, feral fighting men who handled their weapons with experienced and practised ease. All wore coarse puttees, rubber web-toed boots, belted trousers, a bandolier and netting covered, circular-shaped, steel helmets.

Our small party was then herded away along the quay and into a large, dark, musty and hot go-down of a warehouse. Immediately afterwards the large, sliding doors were clanged shut and we heard the Japanese fiddling with the bolts. There were no windows and only the faintest indication of light from a row of fanlights in the roof. Being the only officer present, I felt it incumbent on me to take charge and all I could think of was to ask everyone to muster round and give their names and rank, something, I suppose, that I should have done earlier. Soon each one was calling out, Wright - Yeoman of Signals. Maycock - Leading Telegraphist, Rogers - Leading

118

Seaman, Bunce - Marine Knight Able Seaman, Tattershall - Able Seaman, Monk - Leading Steward.......... I asked if anyone was hurt but, apart from bruising and a few cuts, there were fortunately no serious wounds. I was, however, worried about the four wounded men left on board although I naively expected them to be taken to hospital. As time went on, I began to fear the worst when subsequent enquiries failed to elicit any further information as to their fate. Indeed, none of them were ever seen again.

Our most urgent problem was water and we organised ourselves into two search parties to explore the warehouse by working our way round the walls. It was very dark and we kept stumbling over boxes, pieces of rope and tackle until, suddenly, there was a shout from the other side of the warehouse which echoed and reverberated round the walls. Wright, who was in charge of the other party, had found a small, glassed in office in the corner of the warehouse and which we were soon into by forcing the door. There was a small wash basin in the corner with one of the taps giving a small trickle of water. We rifled the drawers of the desk and a small cupboard and someone shouted in triumph when he found a bottle. Unfortunately the contents proved to have the odour of turpentine. We found nothing but loose papers in the cupboard but our most fortunate find was a sack of raw peanuts which we thought at first contained dried beans. Having drunk our fill of water in turns at the wash basin, we stuffed ourselves with the peanuts until our stomachs were full. Afterwards we found a lavatory, the cistern of which did not work. Then we stumbled back along the wall to some bales of jute sacking upon which we collapsed and were soon asleep. Just before I fell asleep, I idly wondered if I should have set a watch but then decided, under the circumstances, that it was hardly necessary.

We remained in this warehouse for four days in the torpor of stale, hot air and utter boredom overtaking our depressing thoughts. I tried to concentrate on each passing hour rather than dwell on the uncertainties of the future but, in this, I was unsuccessful and, as each day passed, I began to fear for ourselves. We had already explored every inch of the building but there was no way out except through the large, heavy door. However the Japanese had not

119

forgotten us. On the second day, they returned and left a bucket of water, some mangoes and cold rice sufficient for a small ration each. On the third day, they only left a bucket of water and thereby we were all initiated into the pangs of hunger which was to become an almost permanent feature of our lives for the next few years.

Soon after the light penetrated through the skylights on the fifth day, there was a loud banging noise and one half of the sliding door was opened and framed in it were the menacing silhouettes of three Japanese soldiers now wearing their soft peaked caps but still armed with rifles and bayonets. They shouted. We stood where we were not understanding their words. Suddenly they were among us hitting out indiscriminately with their rifle butts and shouting, "Currah, currah," herding us to the main door. We immediately formed up and marched off with the three of them marching alongside us.

The going was comparatively easy marching away from the go-down, even if it was hot on the macadamised surface but this soon gave way to a rough, gravel paved road and those of us without shoes immediately began to hobble, the gravel and rough stones digging into the tender soles of our feet. The Japanese guards noticed our predicament and began to laugh but, as soon as they saw our line begin to waver, they began to shout, "Currah, currah." This seemed to be an all purpose expression of displeasure or annoyance. Soon they were hitting us with their rifle butts and I caught a blow on the side of my neck which sent me reeling. At this stage, we all stopped, which was a mistake, for it was merely a signal for them to lose control of themselves and suddenly they were menacing us with their bayonets. They looked ugly and menacing. Obviously this was no posture. We immediately set off again at a steady pace with the stones and the gravel cutting into our feet and, after a while the going became easier as we regained a paved road in a built up area, by which time the feet of the unshod ones in our party were bleeding. There were very few local people about although we caught glimpses of some taking surreptitious looks at us from behind bushes and fences. After about half an hour we came to a square in the centre of the city which was a small fenced park. There were hundreds of Dutch and British servicemen in this fenced off area, staring out over the steel railings while Japanese guards patrolled the perimeter. The gate was opened and we were squeezed in.

Every available inch of grass was taken up with men sitting or standing with one or two sitting in forks of the few trees that were in the park. Every one of them seemed to have a haversack or kit bag and I noticed two R.A.F. flight sergeants sitting on a steel uniform trunk. In contrast, we were half naked, begrimed, unshaven after eight days, half of us unshod and with no possessions whatsoever. For the moment, however, the feel of the soft, dewy grass on our bleeding feet was bliss and we all stood in a group savouring the moment. After a while, I went across to the two R.A.F. sergeants and asked them if there was a British officer in charge. They looked at me curiously and somewhat aggressively without answering my question, then enquired who we were. When I told them, one of the sergeants, a raw-boned red-headed Scotsman said, "Well, well, the Navy's here at last. We thought you'd never get here."

I bridled immediately but refrained from returning the compliment. As my question remained unanswered, I made my way back to the group who were now, miraculously, sharing hot, sweetened tea from two large enamel mugs. As I approached them, Wright introduced me to Able Seaman Harris of Jupiter. He was very obviously a Londoner with a cheerful, narrow cockney face, irrepressible and full of ingenuity. He had 'borrowed' the tea from some Australians who were brewing up what they called hot sweet and filthy in a far corner with a small spirit stove. When Harris had seen us approaching the park, he rightly concluded who we were.

I warmed to Harris immediately. He told us how Electra, firing her guns to the last, had been sunk about an hour after we had been forced to retire from the first phase of the recent battle and how Jupiter had inexplicably blown up about 9pm the same night, at a time when we were still limping towards Soerabaya. The survivors had been scattered but six of them had been picked up by a Japanese destroyer and, like us, brought to Soerabaya two days later. He told us that the prisoners in the park were composed of mainly British and Dutch air force and army personnel but there were some Australian gunners from whom he had obtained the tea. He warned us,

121

unnecessarily so perhaps, to keep any valuables out of sight and said that if we had any money on us, it was still legal tender for buying food from the Javanese. I had about £20 worth of guilders and pounds still wrapped in the condom around my neck and my waterlogged watch, both of which, I now hid in my back pocket.

We remained in the park for the entire day and, as it wore on, the pangs of thirst and hunger began to increase. At one stage, the Japanese had put a barrel of drinking water through the gate but it had all gone before we knew about it. Some men had excavated a rough latrine in one corner but it was soon overflowing with excreta. Clearly there was no-one in charge.

Early next morning after a fitful night on the grass, we were roused by the hoarse shouts of our guards and, about an hour later, there was bedlam as a group of Jap officers entered the park escorted by some venomous looking soldiers with fixed bayonets, wearing their peaked caps with sun flaps rather than steel helmets. One of them started to harangue us in execrable English, the gist of which being that all English were to leave the park and, as we went through the gate, we were to give our name, rank and number to an officious little Jap who had already seated himself at a portable table on the pavement. This process took hours. Each of our names was written down in Japanese characters. We were then lined up in the main road around the square. Realising that those through first were going to have a long, standing wait in the road for the remainder of the day, we delayed our departure for as long as possible by sitting on the grass. Others began to see the wisdom of our tactics as we watched those in the road slowly wilting in the sun and they too settled down to wait. The Japanese realised what we were doing and began running round the park clubbing everyone within reach with shouts of 'Damme, damme,' which we took to be another expression of annoyance. Unfortunately some of the Dutch who had been told to wait, came in for a share of the clubbing and were shouting, 'not English, not English,' back at the Japs.

At about 3pm the long trail of British prisoners were marched off leaving the park about a quarter full with Dutch and Javanese prisoners. We marched until sunset. Those of us without shoes had taken the precaution of borrowing razor blades and cutting the legs out of our long trousers and wrapping our feet with the material. Soon they were in tatters but the going improved as we marched along a sandy, palm shaded road westward out of Soerabaya and through many kampongs and paddy fields. We eventually arrived at a group of buildings which we subsequently discovered was an agricultural school. There was an airfield nearby to the north and we saw aircraft taking off and landing at frequent intervals. We found a large contingent of British already ensconced and, to our surprise, we found ourselves back into a service milieu of officers and men, orderly duties, working parties, dinner in the mess and service discipline.

The senior British officer was an R.A.F. Wing Commander and the Adjutant was a Flight Lieutenant with a DFC ribbon. There were about thirty officers amongst the five hundred new arrivals and the Wing Commander made a point of interviewing each of us in turn. The camp had, in fact, only been established a few days earlier but there was a reassuring air of military efficiency about his office, in and around which a squad of orderlies marched to and fro, saluting and stamping their feet. It was difficult to realise that this was a Prisoner of War camp.

The Wing Commander himself was an inspiring man with a commanding presence. When I introduced myself as Midshipman Percy, Royal Naval Reserve, he merely smiled and said the correct form of address was Mr Percy, Midshipman as was customary for all officers below a certain rank. While I was being lectured on the need to keep service discipline with regard to dress and punctuality and to keep our minds occupied, he kept his eyes averted from me. I was still clad in the clothes that I had been wearing when I left the Exeter some nine days ago. He then went on to say that the Japanese had almost been overwhelmed by the number of prisoners who had unexpectedly fallen into their hands in Java, virtually without a fight, he was sorry to say. He had also agreed with the Japanese Command to adhere to a temporary containment of all Allied prisoners until such time as they were able to organise a prisoner-of-war administration themselves. It all sounded delightfully gentlemanly, orderly and even chivalrous. He partly confirmed this when he said that the Japanese had been most courteous but would, nevertheless, be extremely firm with anyone who tried to escape or tried sabotaging their presence. The cease fire and surrender of Java had been ordered by the Dutch General who had succeeded General Wavell and had come into effect a few days earlier and nominal rolls of all prisoners in the camp had already been drawn up and presented to the Japanese. It was therefore too late to break away and join isolated groups hiding in the interior and anyone doing so would be treated as an escaped prisoner-of-war upon recapture. He said that in such an event, the treatment would be harsh indeed and warned that there were to be no madcap escape attempts which would endanger the lives of others. He felt it made more sense for us to sit tight until the Allies invaded and took Java, which could only be a matter of time. He, like all of us, had no idea just how long this would eventually prove to be.

He also spoke of my own personal situation. I was apparently one of only a few naval officers in the camp and, by far, the youngest and he was a little puzzled as to where a midshipman ranked. He eventually decided I should rank as the equivalent to an acting pilot officer for purposes of the camp which was about as near as one could get in the R.A.F. but, in effect, meant I was the absolute junior and would remain so. I had half expected to find many other survivors of Exeter in this camp but there were none and it was only years later that I learned that most of them had been landed at Macassar in the Celebes from whence the Captain and several other officers had later been transported to Japan.

That same afternoon, an R.A.F. sergeant found me and, out of a kit bag, he produced a number of khaki tunics and trousers for me to try on together with two or three pairs of good shoes, underclothes and an R.A.F. officer's cap. I eventually equipped myself with a khaki uniform, a pair of shoes and a cap but I removed the R.A.F. officer's badge and handed it back to him. He seemed to take offence at this but was mollified, also somewhat puzzled, when I said I could not wear it because I was not entitled to. By this time, I had also been provided with bedding, shaving gear, towel and soap and even cigarettes, the first I had had for over a week which caused a nauseating light headedness when I lit one up.

Having had a shower and my cut feet cleaned and treated, shaved and dressed in clean clothes again, I felt a warm feeling of well being and went off to search out the Exeters and Jupiters to make sure that they had also received some clothes. I found them newly clothed, well organised in a tight group and having already formed their own mess. They were like all sailors, extremely conservative and somewhat disgruntled at having to dress, as they put it, like a lot of pongoes. But otherwise, they were well on the way to becoming arch prisoners-of-war and had amassed a considerable amount of information about the camp, the inmates and the local surroundings. At that time, we were incredibly allowed out of camp into the nearby town where there were shops selling basic necessities. One seaman had managed to buy some beer and Wright told me a few days later that some had even found willing female companions. There were still a number of Dutch civilians going unconcernedly about their business as if nothing had happened and the local people were keen to barter or trade for food.

As I made my way back to my quarters which I shared with two older RAFVR Flying Officers, I revelled in our new surroundings and thought that a short period of incarceration here would prove to be reasonably enjoyable. I began to make plans to join one or two of the study groups which were in the process of being organised, anything from water colour painting to Japanese, from Dutch to mediaeval history or to join in the many sporting activities from cricket to rugby or football. The food was reasonably good and most officers seemed to have their own private supply of whisky or Dutch schnapps. We expected to stay there for a short time only as every day brought rumours of impending counter invasion by the allies – 'stands to reason, old boy, our side has been immeasurably strengthened by the Americans joining the war and the Japs have quite obviously overstretched themselves far too quickly. Just a matter of arithmetic and time,' or so the discussion went on quite forgetting the important German side of the equation. Even though I was one of the few among the officers who had seen action against the Japanese, a fact which in itself and, because of my youth, did not put me in great favour with some of my elders who had not and had learned to stand somewhat in awe of Japanese skill and with some nagging, worrying doubts on the competence of some of our flag officers. I was nevertheless, a willing victim of the euphoria.

Those early weeks of captivity were traumatic in as much as everyone was still in a state of delayed shock from the swiftness of events which had befallen not only our country's fortunes but our own personal ones as well. Many men still possessed money or valuables and these were put to good use in bartering or purchasing food or other material possessions either from inside or outside the camp. This soon led to the formation of rackets and gangs of comparatively well-off prisoners who stimulated jealousy, bickering and, on one occasion, violence in a sudden outburst of fisticuffs. These activities soon provoked action from the British Officer who decreed that all valuables were to be registered, banned all private trading and established a specially elected group of officers empowered to carry out purchases and barter to ensure an equitable distribution of additional food, particularly for the sick who were in no position to fend for themselves. Enforcement of these regulations among the now heterogeneous group of prisoners was difficult and revolts often broke out which were required to be put down with firmness and tact in the absence of the coercive power of King's regulations. Legally we were subject to the laws of the Japanese and this too was invoked by certain prisoners when faced with disciplinary measures from our own officers.

"Why should I care a bugger about them silly, bloody officers who never did a bleeding thing for me? It's the fucking Japanese that are the bosses now and why should we listen to them. The war is over for us and it's every man for himself, and God for all of us," was a frequent refrain.

As time went on however and adversity closed our ranks, less and less of this refrain was heard but, at the time, it made things difficult for everyone. Perhaps it was for this reason that the Japanese were content to leave us largely to our own devices, divided and weak.

Even to this day, there is no provision within Queen's regulations which may guide the conduct of officers and men who find themselves as Prisoners-of-war, save the general instruction, 'not to divulge to the enemy any information except name, rank and number.' This injunction hardly covers the problem of maintenance of discipline by the officers and N.C.O.s, a few of whom were well equipped to lead by personal example, not always adhering to the principles of 'no privilege without responsibility'. For many prisoners-of-war, this problem never arose as officers and men were often segregated into different camps.

In our case, we remained with the men while our privileges were nominal. A high price was exacted for them when the Japanese commenced a system of punishing officers either individually or collectively for any dereliction of duty on the part of the men. This punishment of the officers by the Japanese seemed to be founded on some ill-reasoned premise that it would perhaps drive a wedge between them and the men. If so, it had the opposite effect to that which was intended for it only confirmed to the men that their officers had not abandoned them. This, in time, welded all of us, officers and men into an effective passive opposition to the Japanese but there were always some who failed to see the advantage of this and continued their sullen rebellion under a two tiered system of authority. Many of these men did not survive, nor did many of the officers who failed to heed the adage, 'look after your horses, your men and only then, yourselves,' and earned the opprobrium of the men, their fellow officers and, in some cases, of themselves, to finally sink into oblivion.

Leadership was not, however, the prerogative of the officers for there were to emerge from the ranks men with outstanding powers of endurance and leadership. There were men like Battery Sergeant Major Hancock of the Royal Artillery who retained a parade ground manner and smartness to the extent that many of us wondered if he realised he was a prisoner-of-war and not back in Woolwich; men like Corporal Batty of the R.A.F. who was everywhere, knew everyone and was always one jump ahead of the Japanese. There were many who were not leaders but each, in their own way, made a contribution. There was a medical orderly who nursed the sick with compassion and whom no man ever mocked for his effeminate manners. There were also the eccentrics, the dreamers, the jesters, the practical jokers, the clever artisans, the grumblers, the malingerers, the scroungers, the card sharps, artists, writers, poets and even the whimsical like the pilot officer who was always writing official letters of complaint to the Commandant which read, 'Sir, I have the honour to bring to your notice the lack of adequate food supplies – or medical supplies – or harassment by the guards' or whatever it was that had sparked his ire that day and 'request herewith that these matters be corrected'. Fortunately for him, he never delivered them but some were a delight to read and laugh about. When paper ran out, he would compose them aloud until, one day on Horuko, he died. There were men like Pendleton with the hunched antagonism of a left-wing student, always preaching Marx to whom we listened but remained unconverted; Clough, handsome, gay and debonair whose careful public school accent finally shattered into a cringing whine and who was to die in mysterious circumstances; Hartshorn, the untidy, cheerful Australian scrounger; Pilgrim, a regular army officer, soft spoken with steel nerves who went blind on Horuko; McLeod, pedantic and argumentative who one day, inexplicably, said quietly, "I've had enough," and was found dead within a few days; Simpson the tough Glaswegian who looked after himself and survived and O'Keefe who always looked after himself and did not. There was Humphrey Place who was almost permanently ill with every known tropical disease in turn who was beaten insensible by a Korean guard to the point of death, endured two long periods of solitary confinement and yet survived and Van Velsen, a tall spare Dutch lieutenant and anthropologist who had an intimate knowledge of the thousand or so tribes of the East Indies but, sadly, never did understand the Japanese.

My two room companions were interesting men. They had been in colonial service in Malaya, commissioned into the RAFVR in Singapore at the beginning of January and sent to Java soon afterwards. James Marsh, the elder of the two, was about thirty seven years of age with a rough craggy face and a burly build, with settled sophisticated tastes, few doubts or illusions and possessing a fund of stories of an interesting early life. He also destroyed any lingering romantic illusions I may have had about that part of the world. Trevor Latimer, the younger by some five years, well built, fair haired and athletic, had spent much of his life in Rhodesia, educated in England, a former engineer with the Public Works Department in Malaya. He was, in contrast to Marsh, a taciturn and dry man, an iconoclast by nature but one who was to prove to have great reserves of courage and endurance. As one of the few naval officers in camp and, trading on my unique experiences, I tended towards precociousness and soon both of them were forced to put me in my place. It was then I discovered that this was one reason why the Wing Commander had put me to billet with them. The other reason was that they should guide and look after me. There were times when I resented their quiet authority but, only after a close shave with the Japanese camp authorities, did I learn to abide by their good sense and counsel. Latimer was one of the few who did not subscribe to the general euphoria of early liberation but this was founded more on a lugubrious and pessimistic outlook on life rather than any realistic assessment of the facts. But, at that time, we had little fact to go on.

I was fortunate in being quartered with Marsh and Latimer who were, in effect, civilians hastily drafted into uniform with a wide experience of the East. While there were a few more like them, most of the officers were almost equally divided between regulars and wartime commissioned officers. The former tended to be men of high integrity and character with somewhat narrow minds who only unbent when playing sport or activities which they pursued with tireless dedication, whereas the latter were men of varying backgrounds, some of whom were only too anxious to preserve their temporary gentleman status. There were some learned and erudite men among them but the intellectuals were usually found among the men in the ranks who believed that life in the ranks would provide them with a greater measure of freedom and better opportunities to study human behaviour in depth during an interesting period in history and politely refused any attempt to commission them. They were mostly agreeably eccentric, quite in keeping with upper class tradition which they liked to think distinguished them. We also had our share of cranks, one in particular being a Sapper officer who turned out to be a dedicated astrologer forever casting horoscopes. Under the uncertainties of our life, his services were naturally in great demand and he enjoyed great success in combining this dubious talent with an innate shrewdness and judgement of character. However he never did forecast the year that the war would end with any accuracy and, after an incident whereby he had unnecessarily raised the hopes of some men, his public astrological hearings were brought to an abrupt close by the SBO. There was also another officer who claimed to be a spirit medium but as the years went on, this subject became one which many of us dared not enquire into too easily.

As the weeks passed, more and more stragglers were brought into the camp, some singly, some in groups and many in an appalling state after having hidden out in the jungle or having been tortured or maltreated by the Japanese. I made the acquaintance of one of these men, a young gunner subaltern named Hugh Dawson who had once had charge of one of those huge but ineffectual coastal defence guns on Singapore and who had managed to get away with a party in a small boat with only a school atlas to guide them. After a series of hair raising adventures travelling through Sumatra in the course of which many of his companions were to die or were left behind to do so, he and two corporals landed on the west coast of Java. After a further series of adventures, he was captured on the south coast, now alone and delirious with malaria having evaded the Japanese for more than three hundred miles with the help of friendly Chinese. His first stop was at an advanced Japanese Army post where he was badly beaten and made to witness the bayoneting of two Chinese who had helped him while he was suspended from a branch of a tree by thin cord tied to his thumbs and his feet barely touching the ground and then, by way of diversion, being made to kneel on sharp bamboo slats and holding a heavy rock for up to three hours at a time. Despite these harrowing experiences, he was remarkably cheerful although somewhat bemused to find himself still alive and looking somewhat older than his twenty years.

His main preoccupation was why had the Japanese allowed him to live and transferred him to the more benign authority of our camp. He frequently spoke of the idiosyncratic and contradictory behaviour of our captors. I had already ceased to enquire into the underlying motives of bizarre behaviour by the Japanese but Dawson was of a more determined mind to explain these to himself and, in particular, the predilection of the Japanese for the use of the sword or the bayonet when a bullet was more humane and efficient in the despatch of defenceless prisoners. This aspect of behaviour obviously disturbed him for he often brought the subject forward in our many conversations. Was there some primeval demon spirit in the Japanese psyche which demanded to be propitiated with frequent blood-letting by the sword? At that time, we both concluded that was being merely further evidence of their recent emergence from savagery. I was to discover many years later that the reason seemed to be somewhat more prosaic. The Japanese had long been led to believe that the use of the gun was ignoble, a notion introduced by the feudal lords (diamyos) and their retainers (the samurai) for essentially practical reasons. In 1543, the Portuguese introduced their clumsy matchlock into Japan where it was soon improved on to good effect by everyone, samurai and commoners alike in the continuation of a fierce bellicosity which had long been a feature of feudal Japan. Soon however, the samurai became alarmed at the proliferating use of lethal weapons in the hands of commoners.

The spirit of the samurai, they said, was being eroded.

No longer would men be required to defend their honour against equals in face to face combat with the sword of katana as the two-handed, double-edged swords were known but, even worse, for a samurai to be killed by a shot from a gun in the hands of a commoner was perhaps the ultimate disgrace to his honour. There were, of course, even more basic reasons. Guns in the hands of serfs in a feudal society were inimitable to the preservation of the privileged state they enjoyed. So, the despicable gun was banned from Japan for over three hundred years until the late 19th century when the Japanese were forced to acknowledge the outside world and appreciate its potential for furthering political aims abroad. Nevertheless, the sword and its extension the bayonet, remained the favoured weapon for the Japanese for it now conferred a certain traditional ennoblement upon even the commonest and lowliest Japanese private. That every Japanese soldier now considered himself to be a samurai was a notion assiduously cultivated by the Japanese hierarchy, together with its attendant tenets of honour, discipline and blind loyalty to the Emperor.

Those early weeks also induced a certain unreality as we settled down to a pleasant round of lectures, musical concerts, cricket and rugby matches, walks in the country and visits to the nearby town to shop. The Japanese were in evidence but remained in the background, surfacing now and then as a reminder of our true situation. My early blows from their rifle butts were almost forgotten and forgiven. But this unreality was also leading us into dangerous habits of thinking.

One evening, as I stood alone outside our small room, Wright came to speak to me. After some preliminary pleasantries, he disclosed, after enjoining me to great secrecy, that he had been approached by three Australian sergeants who were organising an escape attempt. They had invited Wright to join them and he, in turn, was asked to approach me as their plan ultimately depended on somebody who could navigate. Briefly, the plan was to make for the south coast of Java about a hundred miles away where we would either be taken off or we could commandeer a native prahu. My mind recoiled from this apparently hair- brained scheme but, on further revelation, it seemed to be well founded. Apparently the Australians had, through the agency of some Dutch civilians that they had met in the town, made contact with a group of British and Australians who were still holding out and operating in a coffee plantation of the hill region of Melang, 60 miles south of Soerabaya. This small group had apparently gained the confidence of the local population and had already spirited away a number of important servicemen and civilians by submarine to Australia. Submarines were now scarce, it seemed, and a new plan had been devised involving the seizure of native prahu and sailing away from Java. This plan required at least two sailors, one of whom was to act as a navigator. After listening to

Wright, I impulsively agreed but my heart was thumping in my throat.

I could not sleep that night. My mind kept going back to the blood-chilling consequences should we be caught. I lacked the maturity to fully weigh up the implications of the undertaking and tended to think of it as an escapade, rather like bunking out of school where the only consequence of being caught would be caning. But would the Japanese actually execute us if we were recaptured? We had heard of atrocities committed by them in Malaya and elsewhere as an aftermath of battle and conquest but I really didn't believe that they would actually execute us in cold blood for attempting to escape. But then, the Wing Commander had been quite emphatic on that point, or was he only trying to frighten us?

When I saw Wright a few days later, I told him that we would need a chart of some sort and a compass but, on questioning him, he seemed rather evasive and talked of problems which had arisen. I asked him if he could introduce me to the Australians but he said, unconvincingly, that they already knew me and were happy to have me along.

The following evening, which, by my reckoning was the 25th of March, I went searching for him but the other Exeters said he had gone off somewhere. I thought nothing more of it until the next day when, at the morning roll call parade which was conducted with full military precision, it was discovered that three Australian NCOs, an RAF Flight Sergeant and Wright were missing. At that moment I realised they had gone without me and I suddenly felt inadequate but more relieved than anything. I had, in a way, been tested and not found wanting but concluded that they had decided I was too young and inexperienced and, being an officer, may well have caused problems in leadership. I later found out that the RAF Flight Sergeant was the Scot who had spoken sarcastically to me at the park in Soerabaya and that he was a navigator.

An escape party of five determined non-commissioned officers made much more sense than four of them having the embarrassment of a very young, junior officer along as a sort of mascot who could navigate. Nevertheless, my mind was in a torment for, even though their disappearance had been kept from the Japanese for the moment, the senior officer conducted his own stringent enquiries. I was summoned to his office and questioned about Wright who was considered to be one of my men but I lied and said I knew nothing even if I was probably the only officer on camp who knew of the escape plan and the direction in which they were headed. I feared that if I disclosed what I knew, the SBO just might, under the provisions of his gentlemanly agreement with the Japanese, and in anger at having his orders flouted, inform them. That they had escaped was incontrovertible and he would probably have to inform the Japanese of this, but just how and where I kept secret.

As each day passed and there was no more news, I relaxed, feeling somewhat guilty that I had ever doubted the loyalty of our own SBO. But towards the end of the month, there was sudden flurry of activity in the early morning and the appearance of a large number of Japanese. They were all armed with rifles and evil looking bayonets. They took over the SBO's office. We were paraded and left to stand in the sun for hours with the Japanese closely guarding us. Eventually, the Japanese strafe party took themselves off with a grim and determined air and the SBO, looking decidedly shaken, addressed the parade. He announced that five men had escaped from the camp and had been recaptured by the Japanese. He then said that he knew that it was the duty of everyone to escape if they could under the present circumstances. A clear warning had been given by the Japanese and he could not now expect them to comply with the niceties of international law in the treatment of escaped prisoners. Whilst he had every hope that his representation would mean the observance of proper and recognised procedures in such cases would be heeded, he was not sanguine about these and feared they would suffer the most dire consequences. He also added that we ourselves would forfeit the comparative freedom we had enjoyed so far. With that he dismissed us. We heard afterwards that he had been subjected to a savage bout of slapping in his office for not having reported their absence earlier.

News reached us through the grapevine a few days later that the five had been handed over to Kempetai Headquarters at Soerbaya and, within a few days, had been taken to a coconut grove, made to dig their own graves and then been bayoneted to death in front of an audience of Japanese soldiers.

Maycock, the Exeter leading telegraphist heard the news first and came and told me. I was violently ill and prayed to myself, not only for them, but also as a small thanksgiving for them having replaced me. Unable to contain myself any longer, I told Latimer and Marsh of my involvement and they both roundly castigated me for not having told them earlier. The horror and shock was now compounded by another tormenting thought – had I reported the plan earlier to the SBO they may well have been prevented from carrying it out and would still be alive. Latimer was of the opinion that the whole plan had been ill conceived and that they had bungled it by asking me to join then and then replacing me, thus leaving me with a dangerous secret which, as an officer, I was duty bound to disclose even though I hadn't. It was, I then realised, an impetuous decision that had probably led to a serious underrating of the Japanese. Wright was one of the best of British seamen, tough, quick, alert and competent, a good companion and probably well aware of the dangers. I did not know the Australians but probably, like many I did come to know and admire, were tough, good humoured, resilient and always brave and ready to 'have a go'. They were valiant men and, even if they did replace me with the RAF navigator, I was flattered that they had, perhaps ill-advisedly, asked me to accompany them. The execution of Wright, the RAF navigator and the three Australians proved to be a turning point in our comparatively carefree lives for, soon after, the Japanese presence was reinforced by extra guards and strict confinement to within the fenced area. Within a few days, we were told to prepare ourselves for a move.

Our lives dramatically changed on the 19th of April by the sudden appearance of a convoy of small trucks and a detachment of a different, taller and more bony-faced type of Japanese whom we discovered were, in fact, their Korean lackeys. While perhaps it is hard to imagine anyone more vicious and bestial than the Japanese soldiery as we came to know them, the Koreans were infinitely worse. Having been dominated by Japan for many years, it was as if they now welcomed the opportunity of working off their accumulated frustrations on us. And from the moment of this very first encounter, our little world of make believe, comparative idleness, petty jealousies, quarrels, black marketing and rackets vanished as if they had never existed. As we struggled out of the camp in a long line of men carrying their kit helped along with frequent belts across the back and shoulders by these new masters of ours, Jim Marsh said, "Just as well, I was getting bored with the place. Hope the pubs are still open when we get to wherever we are going."

We marched for about six hours and were eventually brought to a halt outside a prison with broken glass on the high enclosing walls. This prison lay close to the centre of Soerabaya near the main creek. It usually housed a few hundred long term prisoners. They had been moved into a small wing and about one thousand British prisoners were somehow shoe-horned into the space that they had vacated. We were now very much hurich – Japanese for Prisoner-of war – and our lives were suddenly restricted to within severely circumscribed limits which consisted of the barrack room where we lived or the vile, evil smelling drains which served as the latrines which made me gag and vomit every time I was forced to go there. There was also a punishment block of solitary confinement cells. The Exeters and Jupiters managed to stay together and, once again, organised themselves with great rapidity with the help of Harris, even if he was somewhat downcast at the sudden demise of his manifold and lucrative enterprises. Soon after moving in, I resolved to give up smoking as my supply was now running low with little prospect of replenishment and to save me the indignity of searching for matches which had also become scarce. I also resolved to start a new journal.

Officers who are prisoners of war are not normally asked to work but the Japanese insisted that we should. Finally a compromise was reached between them and the SBO whereby only junior officers would do so and they would confine themselves to supervising the work. I was glad about that because it gave me the opportunity of

136

getting away from the conditions in the prison and opened up many possibilities. While some working parties were sent to the nearby airfield, we were taken to a small fishing harbour to the northwest of Soerabaya itself which the Japanese seemed to want to be converted into a base for small patrol craft.

We began by building a breakwater of stones brought to the site by lorries which were ill equipped for the task. They were not dump trucks and each one had to be emptied by hand. When we suggested to the Japs that it would be easier if the lorries ran along the section of breakwater already built and discharged their load at the end, we received a short, 'Nei.' We were therefore required to drag these rocks on wooden sledges, which soon gave out, over the full length of the breakwater, an ever increasing distance. The Japs had realised that we were correct but they were not going to lose face by now agreeing to our suggestion. They then compensated by harrying us with shouts of, 'Speedo, speedo,' a self explanatory term accompanied by blows across the shoulders with either a rifle butt, bamboo stick or baulks of timber. We always seemed to have the same guards and two of them in particular became the bete noire of our lives, one of whom named Fukuye, we immediately nick-named with a similar well-known Anglo-Saxon term. He was one of nature's born tormentors and not only to us. I saw him hitting one of his own men in the same way one day.

But there were compensations. The little village was picturesque and we all found opportunities to slip into warm, clear water while working in the heat of the day. Men would also find excuses to sidle off into the surrounding palms and mango trees behind shacks, ostensibly to banjo but really to pick mangoes or to meet their old camp followers of local Chinese who always had fresh fruit, sweets and cigarettes for sale or to barter. Frequently they gave these things to us as presents. These people were accompanied by Dutch women on two occasions who were in considerable danger from the Japanese but, nevertheless, persisted in their visits which did much for our morale. We gleaned snippets of news from them which not only consisted of widely optimistic rumours but also about how the grip of the Japanese was being tightened on everyone in Java.

137

Fukuye's soul mate, Chimasu, who, inexplicably, knew some English, was very tall for a Japanese but we soon found out that he was in fact Korean and had assumed a Japanese name. He was known as Number one which was derived from an incident when, in rare good humour and in an attempt to use his English on a group of seamen prisoners, he said, "Nippon number one – King Georgu number ten out of ten," to which all the prisoners nodded and agreed that 'King Georgu was number ten out of ten.' This obviously caused him some puzzlement as to how we could be so blatantly disrespectful to our King and probably he decided that we were nothing but a traitorous lot. Poor Chimasu, he never did see the point of our jokes although we were unfortunately always the butt of his, which, more often than not, were pathologically cruel. One of his more engaging past-times was to toss stray cats into the air and endeavour to impale them on his bayonet. He invariably missed, I am glad to say.

After we had been working on the breakwater for a backbreaking month, the task getting heavier as it reached further into the sea, we had the first of a long series of incidents. One day, as I was helping some Exeters place some stones near the water level, there was a sudden yell of outrage – 'bugero, bugero,' (idiot) from Fukuye and I saw him beating one of the RAF men with a piece of timber. We had all stopped working to look when Latimer who was in charge of one of the other work parties, ran over and tried to wrest the club from Fukuye's hands. Almost immediately, Latimer was pinned to the ground by other Japanese guards who had run up by now to assist and began to beat him in the most ferocious display of bad temper that we had ever seen. They then dragged him to his feet and ordered the three hundred of us to assemble and return to the prison. They kept us there while Fukuye worked himself up into the most volcanic rage. All the others, about a dozen of us including myself, were then lined up and both Fukuye and Number One began to slap us round the face each in turn. Slap is perhaps a misnomer for this highly diverting form of Japanese assault for it was, more correctly, an open handed blow which sent one reeling, causing the face to swell and usually leaving a bruise. After this, we were all sent back among

138

renewed shouts and yells. Latimer's face by this time was a bloody mess and he seemed to have lost some teeth as I helped him bathe his face in the sea. When we returned to the prison, Latimer was thrown into solitary confinement, where he was subjected to more beatings and ill treatment. After a week, he returned to us, bruised, bleeding and raging silently within himself.

As time went on, the benefits of Japanese culture were also impressed upon us. We discovered that we were now in the fifth month of the fiftieth year of the Showa epoch and not in May 1942. Ironically Showa means peace and enlightenment and was the name chosen by Emperor Hirohito to signify the year starting with his accession to the throne. Clocks were also set by Tokyo time, about one and half hours ahead of Java time, which was merely a daylight saving ruse which meant the working day was stretched by at least two hours. We were also required to give the Japanese military salute. When a Japanese appeared in a building or compound, the nearest prisoner would shout, 'kiutske' (attention), then 'Kiri' (bow), then 'nauri' (straighten up and 'jasmi' (dismiss) and many were the times when a Jap would suddenly appear without warning and those nearest would receive a beating for failing to show respect. One Australian would often mutter under his breath, "Oh, my bloody aching back," as he straightened up.

Our diet was insufficient to meet the demands of the heavy work that we were required to do. This included the officers, for many were now giving helping hands to the men and, within about three months, our figures had all become sylph like. Although we did not know it, we were at that time, comparatively well off, being able to barter or buy food from the Javanese. We managed to get duck, eggs, fruit, vegetables and, sometimes, buffalo meat and thus we were ensured of a small intake of essential vitamins which helped to ward off illness.

However, during the latter part of June, I went down with amoebic dysentery and was removed from my cell to a store room which had been converted into a ward for dysentery patients, fortunately near the drainage pits which served as banjos.

At that time, the medical staff still had supplies of emetime, a specific for amoebic dysentery derived from ipecacuanha and I was given a course of injections. These supplies were soon exhausted and there was nothing the doctors could do except hope that the patient would recover. Dysentery became the major killer of prisoners-of-war and infections soon spread in the conditions in which we lived. One of the doctors, a New Zealander, gave us frequent lectures on preventive health measures in an attempt to lessen the spread of infections and, although we tried and cajoled others, the incidence of infection spread as time passed and our conditions deteriorated. Together with dysentery, there were also frequent out breaks of malaria and dengue or 'breakdown' fever. For the first time, some men were given quinine until supplies ran out, then there was nothing.

Shortly after recovering from my first attack of dysentery, I was afflicted with infected tonsils which gave me a raging temperature, gradually subsiding and leaving me weaker than I had been after the dysentery attack. Because of these bouts of illness, I had not gone out with the working parties and the days were hot and boring, the only distraction being the round of normal duties and a book to re-read over and over again or a game of chess with others who were confined to camp. By the end of July, a reaction to prisoner-of-war life set in and I began to sink into nothing. It seemed that nothing would raise my spirits. About this time, some prisoners either built or smuggled in a radio and we were now receiving regular news reports relayed either from Australia or India which did much to lessen our sense of complete isolation from the outside world. However and perhaps perversely, these reports only served to increase my depression as news of fighting in the Solomon Islands, New Guinea and then Burma and the Indian border reached us. What the Japanese had been saying was indeed true but, more importantly, I realised the staggering extent of the Japanese advance and that there were unlikely to be any liberating armies on their way to Java in the near or distant future.

The Japanese suspected the presence of a radio in the camp when a prisoner in a conversation with an over friendly guard had

140

inadvertently disclosed knowledge of recent British successes in North Africa which could only have come from a clandestine radio. Soon afterwards, we were subjected to sudden searches of our cells, our meagre belongings scattered about and a considerable amount of contraband unearthed but the radio was never found and I myself never asked of its whereabouts deeming it safer not to know. Items of news were very often deftly included in the Padre's sermon at Church parade on a Sunday or during educational lectures.

One evening I was confronted by Trevor Latimer and Jim Marsh and lectured on my state of mind. I resented this but gradually, as they talked with understanding and sympathy, I realised I had been indulging myself in an orgy of self-pity and survival under our conditions was indeed a matter of endurance, loyalty and service. Gradually, the gentle but firm lectures of Jim Marsh began to lift me out of these fits of extreme depression and I began to take a renewed interest in my appearance, perhaps obsessionally so, and also in the welfare of the men from the Jupiter and the Exeter for whom I felt a special regard and responsibility. Years later, I was to come to realise that I was too immature to cope with the mental rigour of imprisonment and it was probably for this reason and not disease alone, which was responsible for the high mortality rate among very young prisoners. I was lucky for Jim Marsh provided me with the mental crutch I needed.

Of the sixteen odd seamen prisoners, three had already suffered savage beatings from the guards on working parties and one of them, a stoker named Cotton, had been deliberately burned by a guard who had pushed him into a fire he had made to roast some sweet potatoes whilst on a working party. His face was now badly disfigured from a suppurating burn. A number had contracted dysentery like myself and two had since gone down with malaria. Ministering to the sick and hurt was the ineffable Harris who had turned his acquisitive traits to good accounts by being able to provide all manner of goods and services without apparently any thought of remuneration. On brushing aside our thanks however, he always said, "It's all written down on the slate, mate, and I'll be around to collect when we get home." Some said that he was only joking but there were some of us who thought otherwise.

I returned to going out of camp on working parties in August, this time to the nearby airfield, the breakwater having been completed. I was pleased to get away from the camp but, as we marched out, I noticed how much thinner and weaker everyone had become and their little more than tattered appearance. I managed to stay close to the Exeters in the working party, enlivened by the presence of Harris who continued with the entrepreneurial activities with the local Chinese. His bartering usually brought forth eggs and fruit but, on occasion, we were all asked to help smuggle some vital tool or other contraband into prison, By his example and under his tuition, we, in turn, all became inveterate pilferers and no movable- and sometimes apparently immovable – piece of glass, metal, string, cloth, paper or food escaped our acquisitive fingers. We were all vigorously searched when we returned but the guards, perhaps under orders from the particularly amiable Commander, always allowed us to take in extra food. We generally managed to pass the searches and in retaining the contraband through different ruses and the use of ingenious places of concealment.

I wrote a few lines in my small journal every week, rewrapped it in a piece of oilcloth and buried it in a hiding place which I was certain would never be discovered. But absolute certainty was one thing absent in a Japanese prisoner-of-war camp – a place of constant surprises, contradictions and unpredictable behaviour. By this time, mid September, our living conditions had become even more cramped with the arrival of a group of Dutch prisoners of war. Whilst most of the officers and NCOs were Dutch, the men were Ambinese, Mendonese or Dutch Eurasians, sometimes known as lap-laps, the equivalent of chee-chees in India. Initially we resented this intrusion into our little British world but the Dutch officers, including two doctors, proved to be men with a considerable fund of knowledge and experience and soon became a welcome addition to our coterie. Alas, the same could not be said of their men who seemed only too ready to cringe in front of the Japanese and there were rumours that some of them were informers. The Dutch officers emphatically

142

discounted any such possibility although, a few years later, I came to realise that the Dutch – or the Orang Blanda as the Javanese called them – for all their qualities, knew little of the people whom they had ruled for more than three centuries.

I hid my journal in the usual place a week after the Dutch had arrived, under the corner of a well concealed drainage cover slab but between two bricks of the wall of the manhole. When I returned a week later, it had been removed. Hastily replacing the cover, I returned the next day to make sure but there was no sign of it. With each mounting hour, my apprehension increased because not only was I flouting the direct orders of the Senior British Officer not to keep a diary but the Japanese would, when they were unable to make any sense of my unique shorthand and abbreviations, conclude it to be in some form of code. After a further day of intense apprehension, Marsh, sensing my discomfort, once again taxed me. I told him what had happened but he merely said, "Don't worry," and went off to see the SBO. Later that day he accompanied me to see the Wing Commander who questioned me closely on the contents of the diary, the time and place that I had hidden it and then delivered me a reprimand for disobeying his orders. He dismissed me by saying that we would have to wait and see, but feared I had been informed on by one of our recent arrivals and the Japanese might well be examining it at that moment.

But nothing happened. The Japanese did not send for me and, after a further week, I was able to breathe more easily. It had obviously not fallen into Japanese hands and I concluded that a fellow prisoner had found it and appropriated it for the oil skin wrapper and the thin paper of the pages which would have made good cigarette papers. This was my last attempt to keep a journal and, apart from a written account written up after the war, I have never kept one since. There are many things in life that are perhaps left best unrecorded.

Although we could be forgiven for not realising it at the time, the next six months from September 1942 until April 1943 proved to be the most comfortable time we spent as prisoners-of-war, the time comfortable merely relative to the experience which was shortly to befall the majority of us. We had now settled down to a routine of daily work parties, study groups, concert rehearsals and scrounging. Although there was an increasing number of sick, the major vitamin deficiency diseases arising from a diet of rice had largely been kept at bay through a small but steady supply of fresh fruit, vegetables and eggs from outside. One of the Dutch doctors had also managed to organise a small supply of rice husks and yeast which, when added to the rice prevented outbreaks of pellagra and beri-beri, both deficiency diseases brought about by lack of niacin and thiamine in the diet.

As time passed, we also got used to the Japanese keeping up their usual harassment accompanied by frequent beatings although we had learned to avoid the more obvious of provocations. This was not to say that the Japanese improved for the knowing but merely that we had become more wary and adept, having learned the idiosyncrasies of various individuals in our dealings with them. However we never did get used to their unpredictability and their apparent schizophrenic personalities: for much of the time they would behave fairly benignly but, like some wounded animal, would suddenly turn on some hapless prisoner for an imagined or real slight and beat him senseless with anything they could lay their hands on including their belts. And the next day, the same guard might appear with a banana or some other offering, drawing in his breath and murmuring apologies. But there were some, like our old friends Fukuye and Chimasu whom we learned to permanently loathe and avoid although this was usually difficult owing to their peripatetic habits.

Whilst we all recognised the Japanese to be fellow human beings, it also entered our minds that they resented this assumption. They seemed determined to be different, the full extent of which only dawning on us after some time. Whereas we were heirs to a system of precise logic and axioms, definitions and proofs leading to definite conclusions, the Japanese were born dialecticians whereby they held that any existence was a contradiction. They instinctively practiced the concept of the contradiction of opposites and the means of harmonizing them, thus leading them to believe that a thing could be both bad and good at the same time. Whereas we tended to think in terms of clear distinction or in black and white, the Japanese mind seemed to inhabit the vast grey area of vaguer instinction and contradiction. They could be polite and barbarous, brave and cowardly, efficient and yet strangely improvident, industrious and lazy or honest and treacherous. To the Japanese, these were not anomalies of behaviour but one united whole and were often puzzled by our lack of understanding of such a simple concept of behaviour. To the Japanese, a man without contradiction could not be respected; a man full of contradiction was a deep man and his life all the more richer for the struggle within himself. The philosophy of life stems from Buddhism, a doctrine where all is absorbed in the spaceless, timeless abyss of non-difference where all is vanity and nothing can be differentiated because nothing has an identity. And nobody knows or is responsible for the movement of change, since there is no Creator, God or Fate.

My nineteenth birthday came and went in November unnoticed except by Marsh who had earlier made a note of it. He gave me a small present of a shaving mirror saying gruffly, "Here, this will stop you borrowing mine." Latimer joined in by giving me an egg saying, "Now that you're nineteen, perhaps you will behave like a man instead of one of Fagin's runners." This was a sly reference to a reputation I had earned for once having assisted Harris in pilfering a considerable amount of aluminium and Perspex from a crashed aircraft at the airfield and as the leader of the sailors who had all earned a reputation as resourceful thieves. I was deeply touched and I remember having tears in my eyes. I also remembered my last birthday as we neared the Cape of Good Hope and the sight of the small Arctic tern came back to me. I wondered if it was making its journey again, free and unfettered.

Jim Marsh was twenty years my senior yet, behind a burly, gruff exterior, he was a highly intelligent and sensitive man who worried about his family, a wife and two adolescent daughters whom he had wisely packed off to Australia long before the fall of Malaya. He had been asked to look after me and this he did by treating me as a son and I reciprocated by learning to abide by his counsel. Trevor

Latimer was a different personality. A man of strong principles, he too worried about his wife who was at home in England and whom, from the odd remarks he passed, I took to be the complaining type who never did take to colonial life. Perhaps it was this that had given him a rather cynical outlook with a distrust of others' motives but he remains, nevertheless, one of the bravest men I have ever known.

Our first Christmas in captivity came round and we all tried to make it a festive occasion. With great will power, food from outside was hoarded and those in the art class made decorations and drew Christmas cards. There was the obligatory pantomime which revealed an astonishing amount of talent in the camp. On the night of the performance, the Japanese commandant sat in the middle of the front row and politely grinned throughout and even stood up when we all did to sing 'There'll always be an England' and 'Land of Hope and Glory' and the Dutch sang their national anthem in a flood of tears and emotion. While this was all going on, the other Japanese stood in the shadows and pondering, or perhaps not, on a great spiritual force being manifested in front of their eyes. But, when I turned in that Christmas night, my Christian feelings of goodwill to all men did not extend to the Japanese and I knew, from that moment onwards, however callously sadistic they were towards us, they would never break our spirit. And yet, paradoxically perhaps, when our next Christmas came round, I was praying for a merciful release and for God to forgive our tormentors for it was conceivable that they knew not what they were doing.

Talk of an impending move began to be bruited abroad in late March and early April of 1943. Some had it that we were to be transported to Japan whilst others had it on equally good authority that we were to work on a railway in Siam. These rumours were soon given credence by the sudden mustering of all prisoners for a medical parade and injections. The medical inspection was a perfunctory one with only the obviously lame and injured being rejected. We were also subjected to a whole battery of injections which the Japanese said were prophylactic against malaria and dysentery even if our own doctors maintained there was no such thing. More than half of the

Jupiters and the Exeters including the inestimable Harris were selected as were Jim Marsh and Trevor Latimer.

Earlier on, Harris had engaged a friendly guard in conversation who informed him that we were being moved to a 'goodo campo' over the sea where conditions would be good and there would be more food for all of us. The reason given for the move was, apparently, a severe food shortage in Java, and the Imperial Japanese army were most concerned that we should be provided with an adequate diet. The fact that Java, at that time, was one of the world's foremost food producers did not hold much hope of an improvement elsewhere but, by that time, we had learned to discount these rather euphoric Japanese promises. After some goading by Harris, the guard also agreed that there would be comfort girls, sake and even a cinema to which Harris had said, "It's going to be a laugh a minute, old sport." These transparent and somewhat childish promises by the Japanese were yet another contradictory quirk of their nature. They were never offended by sarcasm nor with sinister import, rather like a chrysanthemum emerging from behind the sword.

While standing in line awaiting my turn, I happened to notice an officer prisoner who had arrived at the prison some weeks beforehand and whose appearance now looked somewhat familiar. Afterwards, I sought him out and discovered that he was an American navy lieutenant and, to our mutual amazement, found him to be one of the ensigns we had entertained on board the Prince of Wales at Placentia Bay some eighteen months previously. I learned from him of the sinking of the Houston in which he had been serving and also the Perth when she too had tried to break out through the Sunda Strait after the Battle of the Java Sea as it had since become known. He had an unusual story to tell. Although most of the survivors had been picked up, he, with a few more seamen, had managed to get ashore on the coast of Java and had boldly made their way eastwards on foot along the coast in the hope of picking up a prahu and sailing it to safety. The Japanese had, by this time however, prohibited the movement of all native boats along this coast and, as death, sickness and exhaustion overtook them, he and the two remaining sailors were finally captured after six months. They only narrowly escaped execution when they were able to convince their captors that they had not yet been captured and could not, therefore, be treated as escapees. He had broken his leg during this adventure which had not been re-set properly and he was left crippled and was therefore unfit for transportation.

I did not see him again, for the next morning, we were paraded with our kit outside the prison. I was surprised to see how much the Jupiters and Exeters had accumulated during the past year considering that they had come ashore almost destitute. This, in no small way, also applied to myself for I now had a heavy rucksack, a Dutch army haversack, water bottle and my blanket roll containing such paraphernalia as eating spoon, torch, shaving mirror, books, paper, pencils and, most importantly, a spare pair of plimsolls, all of which I had accumulated either by purchase or barter over the past year. The Japanese now started to search our kit and soon had a pile of what they considered to be contraband. In my case, they took three books away but left me with the remainder including the two most precious, the Book of Common Prayer and the Oxford Book of Verse. As the searcher could obviously not read English, this was just another example of Japanese bastardy. I would have thought that my torch and mirror would have been seized as more likely to be articles that they could have put to some nefarious use. After a very long day, we were all packed back into the prison for a comfortless night without our bedding. We reassembled early next morning and were organized into detachments or kumis prior to being marched off to Soerabaya docks.

After a long march partly through the city, we reached the docks. Soerabaya had potholed streets, peeling paintwork on some of the more outstanding examples of Dutch architecture and a wary looking population, not much of an advertisement for Greater Asia prosperity now. The Amagi Maru, a vessel of some 3,000 tons awaited us at the docks and some 2,000 British and Dutch prisoners-of-war were marched on board and told to descend into the holds which to us, standing in the sun, appeared to be merely a black void. There were protests and soon everyone took up the clamour while the Japanese, somewhat surprisingly looked on impassively. Jim Marsh was saying, "I am not going down there under any circumstances," leading others to agree with him. A grim looking Japanese officer then appeared on the superstructure, looked down at the now milling mob of prisoners and shouted out, 'orl men downu,' pointing with an ominous thumbs down gesture like some Roman Emperor. At the same moment, the guard moved towards us and began prodding with their bayonets, clubbing with the butts and shouting 'Currah, currah.' There now seemed little point in arguing and we made a move towards the hold.

As we descended down a vertical, temporary ladder into the gloom of the hold, I noticed that rough wooden false decks had been erected around the bulkheads. These had not been designed for Europeans and looked more suited to Japanese and midget ones at that. There was hardly room to turn in them. After much hammering and clanking and the sound of marching feet above us, the sound of the engines suddenly started and we were underway. Some of us could guess our destination although, by this time, any speculation was soon replaced by the anxiety on our chances of survival in this hell hole. For once I was going to find out the truth of the saying, 'tis better to travel than to arrive,' and I fervently prayed for a moratorium of all warlike activities by the Americans or the British hoping there were none of our submarines now nosing their way into these waters.

The heat in the hold was overwhelming and it soon became a dark, foetid, evil-smelling confine of human excreta and sweaty unwashed bodies. Food was dropped to us but, fortunately, the senior officer, an RAF Flight Lieutenant, had foreseen the consequences of this and had already organised matters to ensure that it was immediately impounded and then shared out equally. We had not eaten since the previous day and the only water we had was in our bottles. We dozed all through that night on the hard deck planking. The hatches were opened early next morning and we were allowed out to the latrines in groups of ten. The latrines were nothing more than wooden structures protruding over the stern which soon became fouled by the evident symptoms of dysentery. We were also allowed to fill our water bottles with fresh water but the guards, some of whom we had seen before, were touchy and nervous and a trip to the latrine became a gauntlet of indiscriminate beatings with their rifle butts. I was one of the early ones on deck and noticed that we were heading almost directly eastward into the early morning sun.

The days soon became a blur of discomfort in the molten heat, hunger and boredom with the ever present background of the maddening slow thump-thump of the ship's engine, tempered only by speculation as to our destination and fear of the unknown. For the first seven days I was able to get on deck when, on some occasions, I was attacked for no reason but, nevertheless, noticed that our course remained eastward. Thereafter we were only allowed out every third day because the Japanese guards, probably as bored as we were, now only opened the hatches for a short while each day allowing fewer groups of ten out before shutting them down again. A roster was then organised ensuring that everyone had a turn out on the deck but this, unfortunately, proved to be a dubious pleasure for it meant being terrorised by the vindictive guards. On the other hand, by remaining below, it meant longer periods in the increasing odour of dysentery and unwashed humanity. Incredibly though, not one of the five hundred men in the hold died although many were to do so soon after we arrived. Many of the seamen now had dysentery but the indestructible Harris remained as cheerful and as helpful as he could. On about our third day out, he gave me a small portion of old, stale, cooked sweet potato wrapped in a cloth.

One of the men had a small pocket book atlas with him that the Japanese searchers had overlooked. We tried to estimate our course and distance each day with the aid of a torch. At intervals of a few days at a time, we had remained at anchor during which time we were not allowed on deck and conditions in the hold became intolerable. After the usual clanking and banging, we would set sail again and from the position of the sun as reported by those who could get on deck, it became obvious that we were headed towards either the Celebes or the Moluccan Archipelago, both lesser known quarters of the Dutch East Indies.

Then one day, the ship's engines finally stopped followed by the opening of the hatch, hoarse shouts and a scramble towards the main ladder. Emerging from the hold and blinking like bearded Rip van Winkles in the strong light after three weeks of almost total gloom, we found we were anchored off a small hilly island draped in dark green jungle with a larger island some miles to the west of us.

We had no idea where we were. It seemed like the end of the world or somewhere where the map had run out. We later discovered that this was Horuko Island and the larger island was Ambonia, both lying to the south of the main island, Ceram. It was also the 13th of May which many of us thought to be a most inauspicious date as we looked across the rain darkened sea at the sinister dark green of Horuko. Our superstitious misgivings were to be amply justified and it wasn't long before our new home was being called Horrible Horuko.

We were ferried ashore in pouring rain but were somewhat cheered to find that our Commandant from Soerabaya was still with us and we hoped for a continuation of our previous amicable relationship. However, this somewhat naive expectation was never fulfilled for Kurushina now proved to be a lazy, ineffectual officer who soon abdicated his responsibility to a Sergeant Gunzo Mori and his toady Kasiyama, another Korean who had adopted a Japanese name, and a former interpreter from Soerabaya. Mori-san's problem was that he wanted to be loved by all but, unfortunately, the darker side of his nature unpredictably kept asserting itself, which at times, bordered on wilful murder. Kasiyama was, by contrast, a tiny man of considerable intellectual resource but completely dominated by Mori.

In the pouring rain, our clothes and kit sodden through, we trudged as a cohort of the damned towards what had been described earlier to Harris, the 'goodo campu'. It was neither 'goodo' nor even a 'campu,' set as it was on the slopes of an undrained swamp, ankle deep in mud and water and graced with a few open-sided, dilapidated bamboo huts with tatty atup roofs through which the rain poured unimpeded. As our eyes searched beyond these temporary and abandoned looking structures for something more substantial in the trees and jungle beyond, Jim Marsh, standing next to me, said, "You know, it all depends on how you look at things. An estate agent might, for example, describe it all as a desirable, secluded residential property, well situated on a private tropical island, running water, luxuriant vegetation, twenty four hour gate porters and in need of minor renovation." Jim had always enlivened our lives with his dry and sardonic articulation of our unspoken thoughts but his attempt on this occasion did little but provoke a few hollow laughs, all of us stunned by the depressing, evil miasma which seemed to exude from the mud and the dark green jungle. When we moved into what was optimistically called a hut, we found it to consist of rotten bamboo uprights which had been badly snagged at one end, only half a roof and a floor of split bamboo raised a few inches above the mud by a few bamboo logs laid underneath. To one side was a now waterlogged drainage ditch which, judging from the excreta floating away from it indicated that there had been recent occupants whom I could only think had fled demented into the jungle or had all died. The only remaining occupants were swarms of mosquitoes whining away in the broken eaves.

That first night on the split bamboo floor with the rain pouring through the roof and the endless bites of mosquitoes was a sleepless one. Next morning, however, order of some sort asserted itself and we began to repair the hut and toiled, nearly naked, in the ever persistent rain digging deeper and longer ditches. We barely gained on the increasing flood of water and when we asked the Japanese for tools, our request was refused. However, by the end of the week, some semblance of order had been achieved but we were already exhausted from lack of sleep which had been denied us by the ever present swarms of mosquitoes and a very much reduced ration of rice. It was then that Jim Marsh introduced a new grace before a meagre meal:-

Heavenly Father, bless us
And keep us all alive
There are ten of us for dinner
And not enough for five.

At the same time, dysentery began to rampage through the camp and, within a short time, there was a serious epidemic. After the first

152

week of settling in, we were paraded and divided into two shifts of six hundred men each to begin unrelenting work on a new airfield nearby in almost incessant rain. It seemed to have rained every day and we were soon describing the climate as being divided into two seasons, a short rainy season of four months and the long rains which lasted eight.

This demand only represented about 60 per cent of the men that had been transported to Horuko but, within a week, there were so many ill with dysentery and malaria that the number of so-called fit men was reduced to a stage where it was impossible to fulfil this quota. The Japanese were enraged whereupon Mori came into his own. He paraded all the officers and proceeded to beat each of us in turn with long bamboo pole. After a while he switched to his three inch belt and he proceeded to belabour me until the buckle nearly ripped my ear off. I was absolutely stunned by this onslaught and I could feel the blood running down my face. It was only with the utmost effort that I remained upright. Yet the next day, he approached Trevor Latimer, offered him a cigarette and enquired solicitously after his health. In discussing this later, Latimer opined that Mori was nothing but a pathological maniac.

But I can remember a young pilot officer saying, "Nonsense, the bugger only wants to be loved and just happens to have rather a unique way of going about it."

Jim Marsh, as always, had the last word when he said, "Well, you know what Aristotle said, 'there are some occupations in which it is impossible to remain virtuous.'

If we thought this first episode was by way of being an initiation ceremony, we were mistaken for we suffered three more of these public beatings soon after that and, about a month later, he paraded all the sick to weed out those he thought were malingering. It was both a pitiful and degrading sight, men barely able to stand, wracked in pain with bloody faeces running down their legs with Mori and his faithful lackey, Kasiyama, walking along the lines of men armed with a large stick and hitting those over the head when he felt like it. These blows to the head were not light taps but good hard blows which sent many staggering and some unconscious.

For a while, death was kept at bay by surviving on reserves brought with us but some time in mid-July, men began to die in ever increasing numbers and, for the next fourteen months dysentery, beri-beri, malaria and exhaustion inexorably eroded our ranks. Death now stalked all of us although it was only the mature among us who were not entirely blind to their own mortality. Those of us in our late adolescence or early twenties were unable to grasp the concept of our death, believing that it always happened to the other man. There were burnt out husks of men who slowly turned to the wall and died.

Men interned by the Japanese

There were those with beri-beri who drowned in their own dropiscal fluid in a final seizure of hiccoughs. There were those with dysentery whose bowels suddenly ruptured in a paroxysm of pain and there were those who just went mad.

For those who miraculously escaped illness, life was a continual round of heavy labour – cutting jungle, felling trees and levelling ground whereas for those left behind in camp and who were not completely incapacitated, there was the dismal task of digging graves in the hard coral for the daily toll of dead. The so called healthy were soon afflicted with the symptoms of vitamin deficiency, pellagra, burning feet, loose teeth, diminished eyesight and ulcers. Pellagra was a particularly unpleasant affliction whereby the skin, after taking on a sunburnt hue, would peel and slough off leaving a raw, exposed surface which, unfortunately, was more often around the genitals. I learned much later that the Australians in Thailand called it rice balls. We knew it as the lergy.

Most of us had enjoyed being in a working party before going to Horuko. In Soerabaya it had meant a release from our close confine, opportunities for barter for extra food and the sight and sounds of normal life. But now, isolated and alone on a jungle island and cooped up with a pathological maniac and a mob of subservient and brutal underlings, we suddenly felt our spirits flag. We were at once helplessly infuriated by the torrent of beatings meted out by Mori and indignant at being employed as slaves on work of direct value to the enemy. Clearing jungle does not present many opportunities for sabotage and delaying tactics by ingenious and elementary blunders under the guise of frenetic keenness were often counter productive. Jungle not cleared to day would have to be cleared tomorrow with probably another beating thrown in as well. We feared that one day, we too would be sick men, sooner rather than later, and our end would be starvation on a bamboo slat in the hospital. However, in lending emphasis to this diabolical decision, the Japanese then announced that working men would be given double rations – not from the main store but from the rations of the men who remained in camp. This decision underestimated both our regard for our fellow men and discipline and matters were soon arranged whereby part of the double rations intended for the fit was surreptitiously with-held and passed to the sick. When the prying of the Japanese made this

155

risky, the fit men voluntarily gave part of their ration to pass on to the sick. It took great willpower to forego those few extra mouthfuls, for that is all they were, but we did and many sick men who would have starved to death were thus enabled to live, if only for a short while longer. Not everyone, however agreed with this sharing of rations for there were those who argued that it was better to let the sick die than to let the strong grow weaker at their expense. Fortunately, the adherents to this overloaded lifeboat philosophy were in a minority.

Nevertheless, this point of view was one which always tempted and tested us, plumbing the absolute depths of our characters. Was it not better for the able and fit to keep the overloaded life boat afloat and forget the helpless and drowning who, if taken aboard would only sink us all. For all the unruliness in the British character there is, thankfully, a redeeming reservoir of unselfish charity and mercy which proved to be the salvation of many of us.

Half my ration went to Jim Marsh who was now seriously ill and, whenever I was not working or sleeping, I spent my time with him. He had a raging malarial fever, pellagra and ulcers although he had somehow avoided dysentery. He told me that he had had many attacks of malaria in the past but now his great body seemed to have sagged and his face had a deathly grey pallor. The hospital had earlier been a shambles but under the untiring efforts of a Dr Springer of the Dutch Army Medical Service, conditions slowly improved. There were no drugs and every inch of space was taken up by the sick lying on sacks, on stretchers or on bare bamboo beds with orderlies cleaning up continually and friends of the patients squatting beside them and comforting them as best they could. Harris sometimes accompanied me when I went to see Jim Marsh usually bringing some offering of food composed of boiled sweet potato leaves or some other bitter-tasting vegetable matter. But Marsh did not recover for he then contracted dysentery despite the superhuman efforts of the medical staff in keeping the hospital clean. He was now denied food except for pish-pash, a sort of watery rice gruel and the juice of boiled leaves but, finally, on the 23rd of July 1943, he died. Trevor Latimer and myself were with him when he gave a gasp and there was a spreading pool of blood around him as his bowels breached. I was stunned and unable to speak at the death of this friendly bear of a man. He had been a father to me for more than a year and the sense of loss almost consumed me which, because of my youth, went unsoothed by memories of outlived sorrow.

We buried Jim Marsh that evening in the cemetery behind the camp with ten others who had also died that day. Coffins were sometimes made from crude planking but, more often than not, from bamboo. A Japanese guard always attended to prevent us from escaping although it was difficult to imagine where we would escape to on that island. As I stumbled back to camp by the light of a guttering lamp from that ghastly, sombre place, too overcome to barely walk, the lines of Longfellow came back to me:

> Take them, O grave and let them lie
> Folded upon thy narrow shelves
> As garments by the soul laid by
> And precious only to ourselves.

And what were the Japanese reactions to this daily wastage of human lives? Surely, we reasoned, it was in their interests to see that we were supplied with a modicum of food and medicine to, at least, keep us at work. But it seemed almost as though they were now bent on wilfully allowing us to die to the last man. On one of the many occasions that Squadron Leader Pitts, the Senior British Officer, remonstrated with Kurushima in a repeated, vain appeal to the latter's better nature, he merely received the callous reply that, 'dead is honourable.' On another occasion, the camp was inspected by a Japanese Army doctor, impeccably dressed and armed with an oversized sword intended to send credibility to an otherwise limited intellect. All the officers were paraded and we were told coolly that the dysentery was all our fault. All we needed to do apparently was to keep our finger nails clean and to swat flies.

About a month after Jim Marsh's death, I contracted dysentery again and, with the death toll still rising, resigned myself to death. There seemed to be no escape for very few of those seriously affected seemed to recover. My body was wracked by pain from continual gripping pains in the bowels, a high temperature and the uncomfortable symptoms of pellagra and leg ulcers. For a long time, oblivion seemed to offer an attraction, a long sleep, undisturbed by the Japanese. But I reckoned without the aid of Harris and the remaining Exeters and Jupiters of whom only eleven were still alive. They kept a vigil over me, cleaned me and set up a steady flow of sermons, their own experiences and jokes. Sometimes they remained silent and waved the flies away from my face. Harris appeared at regular intervals to feed me on a strange tasting liquid made from pish-pash, leaves, bamboo shoots and odd tasting pieces of protein about whose origins I did not enquire too closely. He, too, kept up a patter of stories of his life as an orphan at the Arethusa Homes and then into the Navy which was the only life he really knew. I remember him talking about all the ships he had served on, the idiosyncracies of their captains and officers and of some of his wilder runs ashore. One day, he told me that he had learned to hate all naval officers or 'pigs' as he called them, but thought he might just make an exception in my case. When I thanked him, he merely said, "On the slate, Sir."

Somehow I recovered and regained enough strength to leave the hospital. I also vowed to keep myself as scrupulously clean as possible as my only defence against further infection. But this was well nigh impossible in the continuous rain with my superating legs and genitals and dysentery bacteria and amoeba everywhere. I tried however and soon found it becoming an obsession which almost drove Trevor Latimer to distraction.

The days merged into months and we all began to lose track of time as the continuous round of work in ten to twelve hour shifts, harassment from the guards and the ritual beatings by Mori went on unremittingly with disease, starvation and death taking an ever increasing toll. Unchanging heat blurs the senses, enduring greenness stupefies the ability to count the weeks and only now and again would I enquire the date. I functioned like some ghoul, emaciated with a distended stomach, head shaven and dressed in tattered remnants of trousers, battered cap and wooden clogs on my feet, resembling one of Conrad's forced labourers: '......nothing earthly now, nothing but shadows of disease and starvation, lying confusedly in the greenish gloom......'

Absent too was the natural pendulum of the seasons providing a change of perception, a renewal of dreams and hopes for everywhere was the encroaching, dark green, succulent leaves, parasitic flowers, lantan palms with an under carpet of fermenting leaves and dead, fungus ridden wood spawning new growth in almost incessant rain in an extravagant monotony of reproduction out of its decaying matter. Interspersed with my dreams of food and freedom were memories of that voyage from India to England as a boy: Aden with its stark, jagged lunar-landscaped basalt hills, the red sandstone shores of the Sinai and the clean sand of Suez in a rose-pink afternoon light of late winter, all came to mean a desirable place in my mind. Clean, bare, stark and elemental where man stood alone with nothing but the sand, the sun and the sky and where it was perhaps not surprising that he first conceived the notion of monotheism. There could only be one God in such a setting, unfettered by the cloying, musty, claustrophobic monotony of a disordered jungle in which we now lived. Here, the term God forsaken took on a deeper meaning for us.

There was, however, a comfort in ourselves. Men with common interests and outlook were attracted to each other and small groups developed naturally in which our tribulations, jokes, sorrows and our small material resources were shared. With an almost complete absence of material things, the constant semi starvation and recurrent bouts of illness, the benefits of comradeship within each group became something of the greatest value and our strongest sustaining force in adversity. Friendship became a bright light in our lives, valued above all else and even the greedy and selfish changed their habits under the unspoken threat of exclusion into solitude. But if perhaps one may gain the impression that our self help groups were in some way the supreme achievement of true comradeship, self interest was nevertheless a strong underlying motivation. While held together by common interests and a need to maintain a common front in the face of the manifold threats surrounding our lives, we were not, however free from internal stresses and strains. Many were the occasions that I prayed for a release from the inevitable bickering, the lack of privacy, the boredom of listening to repeated stories, rumours, excuses, explanations and bouts of sulks and self pity, even if I myself was perhaps as guilty of these as were others.

Despite the moral support provided by this intense feeling of comradeship with all its imperfections, the mental strain of captivity was perhaps the hardest to bear. Semi starvation and the lack of essential vitamins gradually diminished our inner strength and resignation and despair probably accounted for as many deaths as disease did. Mental deterioration due to starvation was an insidious process, apathy gave way to depression, boredom, an inability to concentrate and lack of self confidence succeeded by frustrations, strong irritations, loss of sense of humour, mistrust, suspicion of each other, resentment and morbid fears with self pity lurking in the corners of the mind, ever ready to appear at the slightest set back or frustration. There were many who felt cheated of life's opportunities and for those who had already served with distinction and loyalty, the years in captivity were particularly galling, convinced that they had been forgotten whilst their contemporaries and juniors were receiving promotion, decorations and a hero's reward. Unlike many other prisoners-of-war including some of those in Japanese hands, we received no Red Cross parcels nor letters from home even though we discovered later that our relatives had been writing to us regularly and as frequently as they were allowed. The isolation and thought of being forgotten or worse, given up for dead, demoralised all of us even though there were times when I day-dreamed of returning home to the pleasure of astonishment and relief which would surely be registered on the faces of my family.

In November, my twentieth birthday passed unnoticed and soon Christmas and a New Year, 1944, dawned, stirring the dead leaves of hope. We had little news of the outside world but we sensed the war had taken a turning point when, one day, there was an air raid alarm and we saw a number of high flying allied aircraft passing over the island heading northwards. For us, however, life remained unchanged and the early months of the year continued in a blur of working parties, stupefied weariness, beatings, rain, mosquitoes, leeches, heat, disease, semi-starvation and death. The dysentery epidemic continued to rage unchecked and, at one time, there were 1,300 men, more than half the original workforce, too ill to work. This brought fresh forays against us from Mori and his guards and it now did seem that the Japanese had decided to finish us off for good or, at least, allow us to die in a quagmire of disease and exhaustion. Credence was lent to this chilling prospect when Mori announced one day, through his familiar Kasiyama, that there were plenty more prisoners and it didn't matter if we all died. At about this time, Mori surpassed himself when he appeared drunk at one of the almost nightly funerals. As he stood swaying at the grave side and shouting abuse with loud belches, I had an overwhelming desire to push him in, but suddenly he leant over and was silently ill over the corpse as it lay in the open grave. We were at once thunderstruck and disgusted by this sacrilege and Mori never knew how close he came to being torn to death by those of us who watched in a seething, suicidal rage. As it was, we had to restrain the friend of the dead man who shouted, "I'll see you in hell, you dirty, rotten bastard."

Fortunately Mori neither heard nor understood.

Through all this frightfulness we nevertheless maintained a semblance of discipline and every officer had his set duties to perform – with the working parties, supervising burials or as an orderly officer making up lists of these parties, recording the deaths or, saddest of all, collecting and distributing the meagre effects of those who had died. And Mori was always on hand to administer public beatings to all officers as a collective punishment for any supposed dereliction or infringement of the rules by the men. While the officers were thus held responsible, it was the senior British officer who bore the brunt of these punishments. On one occasion, the Japanese decided to issue all of us with boots which had been made for smaller Japanese feet and would not fit those of the Europeans. Mori took this as further evidence of our stubbornness and insubordination and administered a public beating of the SBO, slapping him viciously more than a dozen times. Perhaps the bravest men I knew during my time as a prisoner were such officers as Squadron Leader Pitts who had the misfortune to find themselves the

161

senior British officer in the camp. Their job carried immense responsibility for it was they who took the brunt of the Japanese brutality, were constantly beaten, degraded and frequently called on to make appalling decisions. If they stood up to the Japanese, they were beaten or saw groups of their men chosen for punishment until they relented. If they kow-towed to the Japanese and allowed them full licence to impose intolerable conditions without protest, they were derided and despised as a coward by their own men. That the Japanese did impose intolerable conditions on us at Horuko was, however, no reflection on Squadron Leader Pitt's efforts on our behalf for he consistently badgered the Japanese at great personal risk to himself, employing as his only weapon the force of his own character.

There was a Homeric quality in the courage displayed by our senior officers who might well have addressed us as Ulysses did to his men at Ithaca in Tennyson's poem –

'We are not now that strength which in old days
Moved earth and heaven: that which we are, we are:
One equal temper of heroic hearts
Made weak by time and fate, but strong in will
To strive, to seek, to find and not to yield.'

Not to yield – neither to the Japanese nor ourselves, each of which demanded a different sort of courage. The summoning of courage to wake each day in weakness, hunger and disease to face another endless, heat-laden day of toil; to be able to turn a cheerful face to ones companions; to give away precious food to a friend in greater need and to face the despair of each day without losing a hold on life. Was this sort of courage any different to knights fighting a duel for the sake of honour or the mettle of a soldier in the face of the enemy? Whatever the difference, I believe ours was, nevertheless, more demanding for it needed to be summoned each and every day of our lives. As T.E. Lawrence once remarked, 'Courage is like a bank account. You keep on cashing cheques until, one day, you suddenly find yourself overdrawn.' Many who died of despair were those who suddenly found themselves overdrawn after years of struggle and, in this, I was perhaps fortunate because, pursuing Lawrence's simile further, there were friends with greater reserves than mine who were able to provide me with a 'loan' in a number of 'overdrawn' moments. It was the courage of the few that sustained and inspired those of us less well endowed for courage is less than universal. We were also encouraged by the belief that we were, as a group, more personally courageous than the Japanese who had invested themselves with a fanatic adherence to a despotic system which demanded an obedient, mindless, savage bravery, but not the courage to face the prospect of captivity nor the free-will to question the disgrace which they had been led to believe that this would bring.

Perhaps the most enterprising men of all were the doctors. They had no medicine nor drugs but made preparations from herbs and ingeniously fashioned instruments from pieces of glass or metal. They, too, were often ill, but never once did they begrudge their time to attend to the sick or dying men. Their task was often heart breaking as they watched men die for the want of a handful of simple medicines or vitamins which the Japanese consistently refused to give them.

In July 1944, when the work was almost complete, the Japanese announced that the camp was to be broken up and all prisoners transferred to Ambiona Island. We were taken to a camp at a place called Weijama, flanked by green jungle and rhododendron clad hills and already holding a large number of British, Dutch and Australian prisoners of war where conditions were marginally better. Ambiona Island was heavily populated, intensely cultivated with clove plantations and was one of the more progressive centres within the Dutch East Indies with a long history of European colonisation. These islands were the true Spice Islands and were first settled by the Portuguese during the 16th century followed by the English. It was the Dutch who worked their East India Company as an aid to the state in financing its war of independence against Spain as a contributor to the creation of sea power and as a wealth producer for the nation. And, for more than half a century, they were highly successful. They soon ousted the Portuguese from all the controlling

163

points of Indonesia and, by superior energy and weightier investment, they prevented the English from sharing the spoils. The end of this competition came in 1623 when the English factors or senior merchants in the nearby port of Ambon were executed by the Dutch on a charge of conspiring with the natives against them which, fifty years later, became Dryden's epic drama, Amboyna. It was also here that Alfred Russell Wallace, the English naturalist, experienced his flash of intellectual light which led him to formulate, contemporaneously with Darwin in 1856, the theory of evolution and natural selection.

Now, in these once fabled islands and scene of such ancient, deadly rivalry, the Dutch and the British found themselves victims of an entirely different type of competitor. One is perhaps tempted to say that we were the living proof of Darwin's and Wallace's theory of natural selection, summarised as 'the survival of the fittest,' but this is tautology. The fittest are those that survive, there being no independent criteria of fitness.

Even though our conditions on Ambiona improved with access to slightly increased supplies of food from clandestine sources, Trevor Latimer went down with beri-beri which developed into dropsy or wet beri-beri giving him a grotesque swollen appearance. I tried to obtain some rice bran from a nervous Dutch officer who seemed to have a secret outside supply line organised but I was unsuccessful as I was with other attempts to find some source of vitamin B for him. However, we did discover what I still consider a good, useful preventative against dysentery when, in conversation with a Dutch naval officer, I learned that papaya seeds, small black circular pips found in larger numbers in the centre of each fruit, were often used by the natives. I mentioned this to one of the doctors who agreed that the papien contained in the seeds was a useful herbal remedy for any intestinal complaints but said, "First you find your papaya." This we did by spreading the word to barter for papaya above all else and soon we had a small supply. Although many of us, including myself, were yet to be stricken with further attacks, there were many who swore to their prophylactic powers. The problem lay in securing a supply and this proved difficult and erratic as we soon found out that Ambionia had earned an evil reputation for summary executions by the Japanese for trivial offences which included trading for food from the local people.

After some six weeks in the camp, we were suddenly electrified by the sound of aircraft followed by distant explosions when allied aircraft bombed the town of Ambon. Our cautious optimism which had prevailed since we had left Horuko was now replaced by excitement as rumours began to multiply, the common theme of which being our imminent liberation by an Anglo-American landing. We soon began to organise ourselves by drawing up contingency plans should the Allies invade Ambiona which the bombing seemed to presage. These plans did not include, however, how we would welcome our liberators but how we should avoid being massacred by the Japanese which would surely follow an Allied attempt at landing.

Alas, we were soon to find out that endurance has no limits, the mind, ever ready to move over and make room for each new despair.

It was about the 15th of September when approximately 500 British and Dutch prisoners of war were selected and told to gather their belongings for instant departure. Latimer, like many others, had beri-beri so badly by this time that he could hardly move, his body swollen with fluid and his stomach distended. Nevertheless, we assembled and marched to Ambiona town which was set on the southern side of a narrow westerly facing bay from where we were hurried to the embarkation point along a muddy track. There had been no rain for some time but, on this day, it rained almost continuously turning the track into a glutinous quagmire over the coral. The Korean guards seemed to be as anxious as we were to quit these islands and harried our long column into a shambling trot with hoarse shouts and frequent bashes with their rifle butts. The men suffering from beri-beri were barely able to move but they, too, were pushed and prodded along like cattle. We dared not drop out as rumour spread along the line that the Korean guards were bayoneting all those that did so. Whether or not this was true, we did not attempt to find out. Latimer was being supported by two RAF men just ahead of me and I carried his meagre belongings. Although we had arrived on Horuko with a certain amount of personal kit, our clothes had since rotted and torn, our shoes worn out and most of us were now reduced to wearing rags, loin cloths, or hundoshi, and clogs or even barefoot. All I had of my belongings was a remnant of bedding, two books, Jim Marsh's mirror, razor, spoon, mug and water bottle. Others had far less.

When we finally arrived at the foreshore, we attempted to shelter in some nearby huts but the guards were soon screaming, 'Nei, nei,' at us, forcing us back into line in the open where we stood amid the groans of the sick lying on stretchers in the pouring rain, left to wonder what the hurry was about. In this respect, the Japanese were not dissimilar to the British Army whom, I was told, also indulged in a complex operation known as 'hurry to wait.' We stood there for nearly four hours waiting in the rain until some barges appeared to ferry us to a small ship anchored on the northern side of the bay. As we were towed towards this ship, I was reminded of D.H. Lawrence's lines:

"Pity, oh pity the poor dead that are only ousted from life and crowd there on the grey mud beaches of the margins, gaunt and horrible.

"Waiting, waiting till at last the ancient boatman with the common barge

Shall take them abroad, towards the great goal of oblivion."

Not only were these lines particularly apt but I also wondered whether this small ship, the Maro Maru of about 500 tons with a Javanese crew would indeed take us – the living dead – across some legendary Styx to oblivion or whether another hellish Horuko awaited those of us who would survive this next journey.

When we arrived alongside this ship, it seemed inconceivable that five hundred of us were expected to somehow squeeze into this small coaster. When we hauled the sick and ourselves aboard, we discovered that the hatches were already battened down, the holds being full of cargo and we were expected to travel on deck. A quick mental calculation showed that the deck space available amounted to no more than 1,500 square feet which allowed each man three square feet of space. Apart from this, our total weight would also make the ship dangerously top heavy. At first my mind was divided as to whether to travel on the deck like this or be crammed in the hold but, after our outward journey, I decided that the deck would be preferable. However, we were soon to discover that deck travel brought a different sort of horror under a tropical sun.

Our senior officer was a very able RAF Flight Lieutenant who, although ill, had us organizing the distribution of fit and sick to various spaces on the deck even though it was difficult to find a level space. He protested to the Japanese who finally allowed us to move our kit from the hatch covers and replace them with stretchers of the sick. For the rest of us, it was a matter of standing or, if you were lucky, squatting although we did manage to settle Latimer down in a shaded corner. We were then dismayed by the arrival of a barge alongside full of firewood for the galley stoves which, when brought aboard, filled the decks to the gunwales. This now meant that we had to find standing or squatting room on top of the rough, jagged pieces of wood. At this stage, I prayed that our journey would be a short one to one of the nearby islands even if it was to be another Horuko. Some men said we were returning to Java but, as we had taken seventeen days on our outward journey, I decided it was impossible for one third of our number to return in another ship that was six times smaller. But I was wrong. Adding to these thoughts, our old friends Mori and his Korean familiar, Kasiyama, appeared on board with the guards all of whom were to travel first class in the superstructure. This caused no little alarm for here, in this confined space, we were now entirely and almost literally within Mori's grasp.

Harris and the nine surviving Exeters and Jupiters were with us and it was Harris who told me of the appearance of the 'Heavenly twins.' He said, "In a way, I wouldn't mind this bloody tub being sunk and that bastard Kasiyama to drown – slowly."

When I asked him why he didn't wish for a similar fate for Mori, he said, "Oh, old Mori is alright, he's just a bloody brute and I reckon I've known some Chief Gunner mates who are worse than him."

167

I felt that this was an exaggeration but it held a grain of truth for we all had a perverse and sneaking regard for Mori who, though brutally unpredictable was, nevertheless, an intelligent and straightforward soldier without any meanness about him. Kasiyama, on the other hand, was universally despised and disliked for his toadying to Mori, his slyness and clever facility for mistranslating our words and thus bringing forth cries of rage and a beating from Mori.

Finally we sailed. The sea was rough and, with the increased weight on deck making the ship roll and pitch throughout the night and the seas breaking over the well-deck we stood or crouched and tried to sleep. At dawn the next day, we had our first dead man, a young RAF aircraft man. Soon the tropical sun was beating down on us, parching our lips and slowly broiling the sick and helpless as they lay out on the hatch cover fully exposed to the sun.

On the second day out, men began to die in increasing numbers from exposure and lack of water. The Flight Lieutenant made repeated representations to Mori for an awning to be spread over the hatch area. This was refused but, finally, after about thirty men had died, he relented and a small awning was erected. There were about a score of officers on board and the fit amongst us were given duties which meant moving around the crowded decks by climbing along the gunwale which, in our weakened state, was a precarious operation as the ship rolled and pitched in the swell. Three of us had been given the task of disposing of the dead, collecting and distributing their pitiful belongings to friends and keeping a record from identity discs. I still had my pocket book of Common Prayer from which I read the burial service as we buried the dead over the side but, soon, this was no longer necessary as we came to know the words by heart. As each body was prepared for burial, the Japanese guards helped us by tying a sandbag to the legs to ensure sinking.

The latrines were the usual wooden boxes slung over the side which we tried to keep clean, unfortunately without much success in the uncontrollable results of dysentery coupled with the rolling of the ship. Then, one day, a man fell overboard when attempting to reach the latrine by clambering along the gunwale. Having buried the dead only an hour before, I thought the Japanese would have callously allowed him to drown but, surprisingly, the ship was put about and he was picked up. Any generous thought we might have harboured towards the Japanese for that brief moment were, however, soon dispelled when Mori, in a rage at having seen the ship put about, appeared on deck and summoned all the officers to the superstructure. There we were all beaten by one of the guards with a rope as a punishment for not keeping the men in order. It was a long time before the welts on my back and shoulders disappeared.

After about four days at sea, the ship put in to a place called Raha Moena in the Celebes and here, a new horror awaited us. Soon after anchoring, a junk came alongside with a hundred almost naked and half starved prisoners who were ordered on board. As these men, English and Dutch came over the side, I was aghast at their condition and it was also clear that only by some of us being thrown into the sea could we accommodate them. Somehow though, they were squeezed in and the space for each man was now reduced to a miniscule proportion allowing us only to stand or sit with our knees on our chins on the broken uneven surface of the firewood. These new arrivals were in worse condition than we were, if that was possible, and had recently survived the sinking of another Japanese prison hulk which had been torpedoed by an allied submarine. The senior officer in charge of the party was a Dutch captain who was suffering badly from beri-beri.

We sailed from Raha Moena on a west sou-westerly course across the head of the Gulf of Boni and the confined space on the well-deck soon became one of indescribable horror. Latimer's condition worsened and I managed to have him moved to the hatch cover to take the place of a man who had just died. But the next night, as the pressure of the fluid in his body reached upward to his chest, he began to hiccup loudly and I knew there was nothing more I could do for him. In the early hours of September the 26th he died. We buried him over the side later that morning and I felt suddenly isolated, terribly frightened and alone despite the pressing crush of suffering and dying humanity around me.

For those of us unable to find shade, the days became ones of torment as poor bare skins blistered and ran raw in the sun while our lips blackened from lack of water. We were allowed half a pint of water a day with our meagre ration of rice but, in that sickening heat and exposed to the sun, we required at least four pints of water to prevent dehydration of the body. Adding to our misery we were, one day, treated to the sight of the Korean guards bathing in the barrels of drinking water and splashing it over the deck. At night, the well-deck became a nightmarish place as the hot, humid, tropical air was rent with the hiccups of the dying, the curses of those trying to sleep and the cries of those demented by sunstroke.

Only Harris, Bunce and four other Jupiters and Exeters were still alive at the time of Latimer's death and I began to think that it would not be long before I, too, succumbed. One evening I had a chance to talk to Harris, his small body now almost shrunken to child-like proportions and his small, triangular shaped face dominated by his large, bright blue eyes. He told me that two men had slipped over the side during the previous night in final despair and I wondered how this would be explained to the Japanese who perhaps kept a careful note of the dead in some bestial game of roulette. There was no hope of swimming ashore for those who did slip over the side but the sudden cool balm of the sea enfolding my emaciated and burning body now seemed to hold out an irresistible attraction. For Harris, this journey was but another hardship to be endured and I marvelled at the bright, burning spirit of the man who said vehemently, "I'll not die here and one day I'll go home and die in London."

As I left them, Bunce, his large, emaciated body now looking like some form of praying mantis, asked me how long I thought this would last. As we now seemed to be heading towards Java, I told him that it would probably go on for another week. But, again, I was to be proved wrong.

The ship's engines suddenly stopped one day and, as we lost our way through the water, the ship began to wallow in the slow, glassy swell. We were told that the engines had broken but that we would soon be underway again.

As the hours passed, we remained hove-to, drifting slowly in the heat of the sun and caught in almost breathless air. After a while, the Japanese and the crew were forced to admit that they were unable to repair the engine and volunteers were called for from among the prisoners. Three men, one a naval artificer who had joined us in the Celebes, volunteered and, despite their physical condition, soon had the engines working and we were underway again. After a few more days, during which the horror remained with us as more and more men died, as many as twenty-two on one day, we anchored off the port of Macassar, a large town on the south-western corner of Sulawesi Island in the Celebes, set on the rim of a bay of extraordinary natural beauty.

Those of us who were still fit, a euphemism for any of us that were standing up, were turned to in helping to unload the cargo into lighters. As the hatches were opened, this meant that the sick and dying had to be moved elsewhere and now, utter chaos prevailed. Barely able to move in a sea of bodies, legs and arms, we accomplished this task where we could and passing the cargo from hand to hand. We noted that some of the cargo was ammunition. As the holds were now half empty, we were allowed to move men below where they were shielded from the sun although conditions were just as cramped. On the second day in Macassar, supplies of coconuts, mangoes and cucumbers were brought on board and these were soon rationed out but with dire results for those suffering from dysentery. The last thing a dysentery patient needs is fresh fruit.

We confidently assumed that we would sail shortly in slightly less cramped circumstances but, as each day passed in agonizing heat and boredom without a sign of this happening, we gradually moved to the rim of the unliveable where our whole future became one of hours only. Our minds concentrated on the next pitiful ration of rice or sip of water. Men continued to die and our days and nights were spent ministering to the sick, passing out pitifully small portions of food and water and burying the dead. We remained at Macassar for forty days during which a hundred and fifty men died, an average of four a day. Watching these bodies sink into the deep, clear, still water, their arms moving sideways in some macabre dance of death,

I felt my mind beginning to unhinge. I raged impotently against the Japanese and I decided that Mori and his assistants were not, as we had earlier decided, bent on wilful murder, they were just callously indifferent. Sometimes Mori would look down from the superstructure upon the horror which prevailed on the well-deck. He never seemed to gloat but was merely supremely unconcerned by what he saw.

Was Gunzo Mori, standing there, looking over our heads toward the empty horizon, now pondering the principle of hakho ichui according to which the Japanese were divinely predestined to dominate the world? Did he wear a belt made of a thousand stitches given to him by his womenfolk to preserve his life and ensure his safe return to Nippon or was he happy in the thought that if he died, his ashes would be returned and become immortalised in the Yakasuni Shrine or was he merely musng over those lines of the famous Noringa Motoori – 'If I am asked what is the heart of Japan, I shall reply that it is the fragrance of the wild cherry tree in the rising sun?'

Probably none of those fantasies, but one thing was clear – we, as hurioh, had long forfeited all respect or regard and were beneath contempt in his eyes. For a Japanese to be taken prisoner was the ultimate disgrace which could only be redeemed by death at his own hand, preferably taking one of the enemy with him. By his standards, we had no right to be alive and he was therefore not going to waste food and medicine on men who were without honour and who had not patently done their duty. The fact that they did not keep us alive had, I realised, its own complex reasons. We were a source of slave labour and they were perhaps mildly susceptible to international opinion in their treatment of prisoners but, at the same time, we provided for every Japanese, a deeply rooted psychological need. They all had a strong desire for revenge for centuries of European domination of the East and our humiliation in the degrading and undignified conditions in which we now found ourselves adequately provided for this.

It must have been some time in late October that supplies were taken on board. The Maros Mary weighed anchor and we sailed from

Macassar on a southerly course. Those few of us not otherwise afflicted with illness were, by now, half dead with the heat, exhaustion and boredom, my only solace being my prayer book and book of verse. But neither gave me any real comfort any longer for I had begun to feel that God, who had somehow preserved those of us who were still alive, had now forsaken us. One night, a young man of about my own age and driven out of mental balance by suffering and despair began screaming out a stream of long, blasphemous oaths which were mostly incoherent except for one sentence which he half shouted, 'You desireth not the death of a sinner so please, O God, help me.'

There was no further sound except for the creaking of the ship, the noise of the engines, the sound of the sea and the moans of the sick and dying. Next morning he was dead.

Deliverance did not, however, materialise within a few days as we had hoped, for this ghastly ship now anchored once again off some small, heavily wooded islands to the south of Macassar and where we languished for about another fourteen days. More and more men died at this anchorage and, each day, we buried an ever increasing number of dead as the days and nights emerged into one long macabre dance of death. I then went down with dysentery which I had, by this time, come to accept as my inevitable fate. I had been troubled with incipient diarrhoea for weeks but, one day, I was gripped by severe pains and soon blood and mucus was flowing from me. I retired below into the hold, out of the sun and into a charnel house where the ordure of death and dysentery hung like a miasma in the hot foetid air. And, once again, it was Harris who sought me out and brought me water and rice gruel, badgered one of the Dutch orderlies to keep me clean and cursed himself for not saving some papaya seeds for me. In this confine, my twenty-first birthday passed although I do not remember the day.

The ship sailed after about two weeks and there was a welcome breath of fresh air now being blown into the hold. Perhaps responding on to Harris's entreaty to 'hold on, we'll soon be back in Java,' I improved or, at least, the dysentery got no worse. Soon I was able to eat some solid balls of cold rice but I was unable to sit up, overcome by an infant like weakness. Days afterwards we finally docked at Soerabaya which some of us had come to regard as home and the near naked and tattered human wrecks that we were shuffled ashore under the silent gaze of Mori, Kasiyama and the Korean guards.

I was carried ashore on a stretcher by Bunce and a Dutch soldier but most of us were not only weak from semi-starvation and disease, many had not used their limbs properly for months and when they stepped ashore, they collapsed on the dockside. The Korean guards, having now perhaps recovered from seeing the state of us, now began to belabour us but, because of a growing audience, refrained from threatening us with their bayonets as was their wont. Soon they shouted, 'Yazume-rest,' and we all thankfully sank to the ground. The audience was a strange one and shortly led to a bizarre incident. They were German sailors whom, I could only presume, had come from a German U-boat or armed raider in the harbour although it took us all some time before we realised who they were. Two of them, strong and fit looking men, walked towards Bunce, Harris, the Dutch soldier and myself and asked interrogatively but with some concern, 'Tommy? Tommy?' Harris said somewhat fiercely, "No, we're British."

The Germans laughed and started to hand us sweets and cigarettes and durain fruit from a bag, whereupon there were loud shouts from the end of the dock and three of the guards came rushing up waving their rifles at the Germans. One of them turned and faced the advancing Koreans who froze in their tracks, undecided and muttering amongst themselves while the two Germans, who were now joined by about a dozen of their comrades, stood their ground. Finally the Koreans shrugged and walked away while the Germans laughed to themselves. This was a strange situation for us. We wanted to applaud the Germans but they, too, were our enemies so we kept silent except for the Dutchman who said, 'danke.' This incident did not bode well for us because, no sooner had the Germans walked off, than the Koreans were back with us having brought Mori and Kasiyama as well who now made us pay for the loss of face they had suffered at the hands of the Deutzels, as the Japanese called all

Germans. They soon began to cuff and hit us to our feet with loud shouts of, 'Currah, currah.'

Soon we were moving off in a slow line. I do not remember much of our subsequent journey back to the prison camp. The camp was full of British, Dutch and Australian prisoners of war, many more than there had been when we left. Our arrival caused much consternation and horror amongst them. Apparently there had been strong rumours of more working parties being organised for work in Sumatra at the time of our appearance, like ghouls back from some slimy, sodden graveyard, which completely unnerved the strongest of them and, understandably increased their apprehension. I was later to discover that we had returned to Java on November the 23rd, ten days after my 21st birthday and my 1,020th day in captivity. Our voyage from Ambiona had taken sixty-seven days to cover a distance of 1,200 miles, a speed less than that of walking pace. During the voyage, just over 300 British and Dutch prisoners had died and it was to be later established that of the 2,070 prisoners taken from Java to Horuko in April 1943, only some 900 were still alive at the end of the war. Jim Marsh was buried in a shallow grave on Horuko; Trevor Latimer in the depths of the Gulf of Boni and only seven, including Harris and myself, of the fourteen Jupiters and Exeters returned.

As was to be expected, things had got worse at the camp in Java. The meagre supplies of food from outside had dwindled as prices rose well above the means of any prisoner-of- war unless he had some article of value for barter which, at this stage, was unlikely. Many Chinese however, despite persecution by the Japanese, continued to provide some supplies against promissory notes issued by the senior officers to be redeemed after the war. The Chinese never doubted our ultimate victory. But if they believed as much, there were many in the camp, including the officers, who only foresaw many years of captivity in front of us and held serious doubts as to whether we would survive this term. This assessment was a rational and objective one for, although we had news of the Allied advances against the Japanese, it was clear that the latter were going to contest every yard of jungle and every coral atoll. It was not an encouraging prospect but for the moment at least, there were those of us who were merely happy to be still alive.

The prison was by way of a homecoming. We met many old friends that we had left behind and slipped into a comparatively well-ordered routine which had grown over the years. It now even included a camp newspaper and access to news from the clandestine wireless in the camp. Extra rations were somehow found for the survivors of Horuko and I received half a duck egg for a week and some green vegetable stew in addition to the rice ration. Despite anything we may have felt with regard to the years still ahead of us, I, for one, was immeasurably cheered to hear how the Japanese invasion of India had been halted at Imphal and Kohima and of a new British army moving into Burma and of the Americans in the Pacific who had since landed in the Philipines. Closer to us was the news of British carrier borne aircraft having raided Soerabaya the previous May and soon we heard of another British raid on Palembang in Sumatra which had apparently put an oil refinery out of action. If we gained anything from this news, it was counterbalanced by the unexpected and sudden appearance of Gunzo Mori, Kasiyama and Kurushima in the camp like some smouldering volcano. Mori immediately set about his customary and untiring brutality, revelling in a larger and new found audience.

Physically all of us were changed men, those of us from Horuko more so than the others. There had also been a significant change in mental attitude amongst the English in particular. Gone was our English amateurism expressing itself in muddling through with frivolous, languid and casual attitudes as though being a prisoner-of-war was yet another game to be played fairly and according to some unwritten code of behaviour. Gone was the inability to see things in black and white and only through the blue-greyish haze devised from the misty pale light of our island home. In its place was a certain hardness, a more straightforward honesty towards oneself, towards others and a self-help philosophy. Far from muddling through, there was now a deadly earnestness in staying alive and, as each new indignity was imposed upon us, the firmer our resolve became.

I was ill for two months with recurring dysentery when we returned from Horuko. My legs were still covered in sores and ulcers and my pellagra was still with me, although it had lessened in severity. In our emaciated state, ulcers and raw, abraded skin soon developed on our pelvic bones where these protruded which made sleeping on one's side uncomfortable. Dick Bonser, the American lieutenant who I had met on the day prior to our departure for Horuko, soon became a firm friend and visited me frequently. One day he came limping into the hospital where I lay and handed me a small paper-wrapped packet in which were concealed about two dozen small, brown tablets. These were vitamin B yeast which, he said, he had managed to obtain from some Chinese contacts outside. I immediately began swallowing them and, within a week, I was recovering. Fortunately he was able to obtain further supplies of these from time to time and these, I believe, did much to restore my precarious health and also those of Harris, Bunce and others. Our pellagra began to heal and the symptoms of beri-beri all but receded in most of us.

Although my body now seemed to be regaining some strength, my mind was still filled with the horrors of the journey back from Horuko which, from even such a short distance in time now seemed to have been much worse. This was because our minds were probably numbed at the time by the sight of suffering and death whereby some instinctive, protective device, a carapace had been formed over our conscious minds with only the locomotor parts still functioning. Now, before all these horrors were to be relegated to the subconscious, they somehow needed to be sorted between the various compartments of my mind. I had no nightmares but there were times when I felt my mind would unhinge and I would lose my reason. Fortunately Dick Bonser was a perceptive man and he encouraged me to talk freely of our experience and I began to do so, repeating myself many times, and I began to feel my sanity return. Bonser said later that he had not believed half of what I had told him.

The next three months bringing us into 1945, saw our rations shrink to almost infinitesimal proportions in a land well known for its bounteous yields of food crops brought about by the diligence of the peasant and Dutch agricultural expertise. At the same time, news of allied advances began to reach us with a corresponding change in the behaviour of the Japanese guards. We now began to entertain the thought that the war might end sooner than we had anticipated which brought about what the Japanese might do to us if the war went against them in some catastrophic way. When the news of the German surrender reached us in mid-May, we could hardly contain ourselves from celebrating, but this would have betrayed our clandestine source. However, the Japanese admitted it themselves within days – the Deutzel, they said, was finished but the Nippon would go on for a thousand years. We all now realised that the might of the allies would now be turned on the Japanese and we entered a period of high tension and we discussed the chances of the Allies freeing us before we either starved to death or the Japanese massacred us. For many of us, the very word massacre held an unbelievable quality about it and we shrank from the thought that, after all we had endured, the Japanese would, in the end, have the final say. This threat was to hang over our heads for the remainder of our time as prisoners, clouding our yearnings and causing us to mentally hold our breath in suspense.

Towards the end of June, we were suddenly told to pack and be ready to move. When we heard it rumoured that we were all being sent to one vast camp where all prisoners-of-war were being concentrated, we were filled with apprehension and considerable disquiet. The rumoured threats of a final liquidation of all prisoners-of-war now seemed possible, not daring to admit to ourselves that it could be probable. Within a day of being warned, a long line of emaciated British, Australian, Dutch and Dutch national prisoners marched out of camp. The subsequent journey by train was one of unremitting jolts and bangs, thirst and hunger. I realised I was far from well and slowly succumbing to the very much reduced rations. I frequently felt faint and dizzy from lack of food and, on two occasions, I fainted while standing in wait for either a truck or a train. Somehow we arrived at our new prison at Bandoeng in the central highlands of Java.

Upon arrival, together with many other prisoners from other camps, we were crammed into a prison. This city served as the summer capital of Java, situated as it was on the central plateau which runs as a spine through the country. The air was clear and sparkling after a downpour of rain and, for the first time in just over three years, we were able to savour a climate which, although hot, was free from the suffocating weight of humidity-laden hot air. There was a vibrancy in the air and we were entranced by the jewelled beauty of this plateau, dominated by the perfect summit of Mount Cereme and the high volcano Tangkopeboehan, below which the neat pattern of tea garden terraces stretched away like some dappled green patchwork quilt for as far as the eye could see.

Surrounded now by a world of great physical beauty and attraction, our longing for freedom increased sharply. I dreamt of being able to walk for miles, paddling in some small mountain brook, perhaps dozing on the bank after eating a meal of crusty bread and cheese, perhaps a glass of wine and perhaps a thimbleful of thick, sweet, black coffee. I thought of the lines of Rupert Brooke written in Berlin in 1913:

> God! I will pack and take a train
> And get me to England once again!
> For England's the one land, I know
> Where men with splendid hearts may go.

If the physical world in which we found ourselves held out so much peace and beauty and promise, the prison in which we found ourselves held out only the threat of starvation, disease and possibly death. We were badly overcrowded and, within a few days, I began to experience a claustrophobic panic similar to the one that assailed me on our journey to and from Horuko. However, if I felt crowded in the prison, worse was to follow for, after about ten days, we were suddenly told to gather our belongings in readiness for another move. This time our journey was a short one to another, even smaller prison on the outskirts of Bandoeng where over six thousand British and Dutch prisoners, scooped up from the camps all along the coast, were now crammed into a prison which had been built to house a few hundred juvenile delinquents. The conditions of overcrowding were the worst we had ever been subjected to and even the Japanese who always seemed to lack the quality of being able to estimate the number of men who could fit into a certain space or the amount of food required to keep a small number alive, realised something was amiss and issued us with rough timber to make bunks up each wall. There was insufficient kitchen space to cook even the starvation rations for so many men at once and the latrines had been built to accommodate the daily needs of a few hundred delinquents, never mind six thousand men, most of whom were suffering from dysentery. This became a major feature of our lives as we now seemed to be standing in line for our turn at the latrine for the greater part of the day and night. Fortunately an irrigation ditch ran through the prison and we were soon organised into water carrying parties to keep the latrines continuously flushed and clean which lessened the threat of disease.

Along with junior officers and men of different nationalities, a galaxy of senior officers ranging from Colonels to Wing Commanders had also been concentrated in the camp. There were also a number of Australian and American naval officers from the Perth and Houston and it was from them that I learned that the majority of the Exeters, about 800 in all including Captain Gordon and other senior officers, from whom we had become separated after the sinking, had been landed in Macassar. Among the senior officers in the Bodoeng prison was a South African Lieutenant Colonel, later to become the well known author, Sir Laurens van der Post, and this period of our lives has since been portrayed in his brief but evocative book, 'The Night of the New Moon.' Van der Post, serving in a British regiment had been captured by the Japanese some time after the Java cease fire when he and the small guerrilla band he led had held out in western Java fighting a rearguard action.

There was also a number of Dutch soldiers in the prison and their native troops which included a proportion of Eurasions. From our earlier acquaintance with these men, I noticed that they had not changed their cringing attitude toward the Japanese and, if anything, had become more sycophantic. At the same time, however, I felt some pity for them because they sensed somehow that their world was about to change in which new alliances and allegiances would have to be sought. Furthermore, they knew that while the Japanese were perhaps, at times, reluctant to take extreme measures against the British and other Europeans, they already had sufficient evidence to show how the Japanese regarded all Eurasians. Nevertheless, we were all sure that a number of these Dutch colonial soldiers were informers and, as a result, we remained in small tight-mouthed groups, not daring to exchange news with anyone except those of our immediate circle. As officers, we were given quarters separate from the men although in our overcrowded condition, this was merely a nominal attempt at maintaining internal discipline.

My material life had also improved by this time having been bequeathed a number of small items including a sleeping mat and a mosquito net. Dick Bonser remained a close friend and we both shared everything that came our way. Food rations were pitifully inadequate but a group of officers were allowed to negotiate with local people whereby a small supply of fruit, duck eggs and additional rice found their way into the prison. My physical condition had improved slightly since the nightmare of Horuko and the horrific journey back to Java but the shutters of my mind had by now temporarily closed on the more searing memories to make way for more immediate fears.

We continued to receive daily news broadcasts by the clandestine radio from either India or Australia and these did much to sustain our morale but paradoxically also served to increase our apprehension. We learned of the capture of Iwo Jima and Okinawa by the Americans almost on Japan's door-step and of the British advance towards Rangoon but, at the same time, we realised that as the noose gradually tightened around Japan itself, all the conquered lands of South East Asia would soon become isolated from the centre. It followed that even if Japan herself was to be invaded by the allies, the Japanese in our part of the world would continue to resist to the last man and take us with them in some Samson-like grand finale. They were indeed days of rising tension and expectancy but, curiously, interspersed with days of resignation to whatever fate had in store for us.

These fears were discussed amongst ourselves but I did not then know of the contingency plans which the officers in the camp had already undertaken since recounted by van der Post. These senior officers were much more conscious of the peril than we were, having gleaned some intelligence on the sinister intentions of the Japanese with regard to all prisoners-of-war should the war go against them. Confined as we were within the prison walls, a massacre would have been a simple matter but the senior officers were determined that we should not go down without a fight. Van der Post has described how, under the rules of levelling the uneven parade ground within the prison, the Japanese had been talked into allowing working parties out of the prison to collect stones as paving. Apparently these were to be used as missiles against the Japanese should they attempt to turn their machine guns on us. Some of the fittest men under experienced and reliable officers were also formed into special security squads as a nucleus of a counter attack force. It now seems quite ludicrous that we should have planned such desperate counter measures but it says much for our spirit which, despite all we had been subjected to, convinced us that we could do so.

Working parties were then organised and this gave us a chance to get clear of that bleak, grim prison for a few hours each day. Many grumbled at the pointlessness of gathering stones to pave a parade ground as it smacked of typical British Army bull but then, we were not privy to our senior officers' intentions. Harris, whom I had not seen much of in the previous weeks, was with the working party I had accompanied and he was bitter in his denunciation of our senior officers for apparently agreeing with the Japanese that we should undertake this task. I felt disgruntled too because, although the work would not normally have been onerous, many of us were subsisting on our very last physical reserves and the added exertion did nothing to preserve them. It also rained heavily at the time and we were frequently drenched, losing body heat and energy which we could ill afford. And so, day after day, we carted stones into the prison until the parade ground was completely paved, an unsuspected magazine of missiles under our feet.

At about this time, we heard, through the mysterious grapevine, that the Japanese were organising work parties of civilian internees from the nearby Tjimahi camp to work on the railway in the Tjitjilengka region and that we would be joining them too.

I welcomed this news for most of us did not have enough energy left to survive, far less undertake heavy work and it would release us from this overcrowded, confining, claustrophobic and sinister prison. However, this proved to be a false rumour although it may well have been that events overtook the Japanese intentions in this regard.

At the same time there were demands from the Japanese for technicians and artisans amongst us to work in munitions factories. When such men in our midst professed ignorance in such technical matters and there were no volunteers, the Jaspanese were enraged. The consequence of this particular rage have since been recounted by van der Post whereby all the senior officers, twelve in all, were paraded before Mori and individually beaten. The Senior British Officer, an RAF Wing Commander, was not only slapped but Mori surpassed himself by bringing a wooden chair down on his head in a splintering crash which almost, but not quite, sent him reeling. And then, incredibly, van der Post who had already had his share of the beating walked across and offered himself to Mori for a further beating. His sudden appearance in front of Mori seemed to completely unnerve him, his mind grappling with this unbelievable effrontery, for he then suddenly tired of the proceedings and walked away muttering to himself. This was the last time that Mori held a ritual beating of the officers.

Throughout those final days, I was afflicted by a recurrence of 'burning feet' and for most nights, I stayed awake with my feet immersed in a basin of water against the advice of our doctors, until fatigue overcame pain and I would sink into a fitful doze. During the long hours of the night, I became increasingly aware of the unspoken threat to our existence and my ears became attuned to the slightest sound. Close to were the restless movements of my fellows in fitful sleep, now and then interspersed with incoherent ramblings and loud

183

exhalations, the odd sounds from the Japanese guard house, the crunch of a footfall on the broken stone paving, the distant noise of the wind sighing through the trees and the harsh croaking of frogs in the nearby irrigation ditch. Nothing in the world could have sounded more peaceful and reassuring and yet the sense of danger was everywhere. I was no longer listening for sounds which would herald a sudden mid-night search of our quarters by the guards, but straining for something beyond these night sounds, something, I knew not what, bugle, drums and shouts of rescue perhaps, sinister clicking of rifle bolts and boots or the cocking of a machine gun. In those long quiet hours, the imagination lay open like a wide bay to every swell breaking on the shore of one's conscious mind. The end of our imprisonment seemed nigh and each of us, all six thousand of us, lay expectantly hushed, holding our breaths and sometimes praying.

On the penultimate day of our imprisonment, I went to seek out Harris and Bunce. I needed their calm reassurance on a day which had started normally with dawn tenko and a dispersal to work or lectures where interest soon disintegrated in incessant talk and rumour. I found Harris with a group of British gunners to whom he had become attached and who all greeted me with a quiet calmness and stoicism. My heightened tension soon relaxed in the face of their imperturbable calmness and common sense arguments. A gunner sergeant, a man of about thirty-five with a face seared and burnished by a thousand suns spoke slowly and deliberately, "I reckon the Nips are shit-scared at the moment and this sudden calm doesn't necessarily mean anything sinister. They couldn't hope to shoot us all, take too long for one thing. There are only a few of them and, if the worst comes to the worst, we could, if needs be, rush a machine gun. A lot of chaps will end up as mungaree for the shite-hawks but the majority of us would do for them. No, I reckon Mori and his mates are wondering what to do once it is announced that the war is over. My bet is that, one fine day, we will wake up and find that the whole sodding lot of them have scarpered and we will be left to shift for ourselves."

Harris joined in, "We all think he's right. There's nothing to worry about. The Nips 'ave 'ad it and we'll do for them in the end."

Although considerably relieved by this confident talk, there was, nevertheless, an underlying note of tension in their voices, a sudden involuntary rise in pitch at the end of a sentence.

"Well I don't know," I felt I had to say, "we all know them for their diabolical behaviour and I feel anything could happen. I'm, for one, keeping my powder dry."

They all smiled and, as I looked at each of their faces, I actually felt a wave of strength of the spirit emanate from them. I had never experienced such a feeling before. It was as if I could touch it with my hand and suddenly, I knew that the Japanese had not only lost the war, they had lost the struggle for ascendancy over our spirit, something they had set much store in. However much they despised us as their prisoners of war or resented us as Westerners and erstwhile masters of the East, however much they had starved, degraded, beaten and humiliated us, it was men like this, the ordinary British soldier, sailor and airman who had remained steadfast and unbowed.

Then 21st of August dawned and, after morning tenko, the Japanese announced that there would be no work that day. In the afternoon, a general rumour started that the war was over and we were being moved to the coast that very night. Years later I was to learn how van der Post had been summoned that afternoon and been informed by the Japanese command that the war was indeed over because, as they put it. 'The Emperor of Japan had graciously acceded to repeated requests to cease hostilities and avoid further needless bloodshed.'

But before he had returned to the camp, we had already been told to pack our belongings and confidently expect to be on our way home within a few days, little realising that the Allies were quite unprepared for the sudden collapse of Japan and had, indeed, been girding themselves for a long drawn-out campaign which was to culminate in the invasion of Japan itself in the March of the following year. It would be some weeks yet before enough ships and aircraft would be mobilised to repatriate us.

We marched out of prison to freedom on that Tuesday night first to the station in Bandoeng and then on a slow, clanking train to

Batavia. When we reached the coast, we were marched in the overwhelming heat and humidity once again to what appeared to be a former army barracks where there were now thousands of prisoners-of-war and internees. Arrangements were make-shift and, as more and more prisoners arrived each day, the general air of disorganisation tended to increase. Having been inured to years of making the best of our surroundings, we soon set about organising ourselves into self help groups. Our disappointment at the delay which now seemed to be creeping slowly upon us was, however, alleviated to the extent that the Japanese now released to us quantities of clothing, cigarettes and extra food, much of it with Red Cross markings that had been intended for us. We were also allowed to leave the camp and visit specific areas but the majority of Batavia was out of bounds. The Japanese were still in occupation but it wasn't from them that we expected trouble but rather from the increasing violence of political agitation of various nationalist groups jockeying for power amongst themselves in an effort to take over the Dutch East Indies before the British could take it over and hand it back to the Dutch. The Dutch were highly unpopular and once we were inside the camp, we tended to stay there.

Throughout the whole period of my imprisonment, we were to live and suffer alongside the Dutch and many friendships had been made. There were also some outstanding men among them especially the medical staff who we came to respect and regard highly. But, on the whole, the Dutch were, as a group, obstinate and insensitive. Their pride had been affronted by the fall of the Netherlands to the Germans and this was exacerbated by the awareness among ourselves by the different levels of resistance put to the Japanese by themselves and by the British in Malaysia and the Australians who had fought hard in a rearguard action denying the essential resources of Malaysia to the Japanese whereas the whole of the Dutch East Indies had fallen virtually without a fight. The Dutch are a somewhat proud and prickly people and their ultimate dependence upon the British and Americans in releasing them from bondage in 1945 imposed an additional sense of obligation and lowering of their self esteem. At the same time, this also received a further blow when they realised that the indigenous peoples of their Eastern possessions, no longer wished to resume their lives under Dutch rule. Dutch prestige had probably taken a bigger blow than any of the European powers with the French running a good second. The defeat of their metropolitan centres by the Germans had the direct result of encouraging nationalist aspirations in their possessions in the East whereas Britain, despite a lowering of prestige occasioned by the fall of Singapore, were to emerge in 1945 with greater influence than she had enjoyed at the beginning of the war with her troops in occupation throughout the Far East. To many Dutch, it was bad enough being stripped of their possessions by the Japanese but to now have their former subjects reject a re-imposition of their rule and their commercial rivals, the British, now in the commanding position was galling in the extreme. We had many opportunities in observing the Dutch in relationship with their East Indian and Eurasian troops. They tended to despise their own men and carry over their values and attitudes that they had developed as merchants and colonists into the army with none of the closely-knit family relationships which existed between British and Indian officers and men in the Indian army.

It wasn't long before we were alerted by the news that some British officers and men had landed and were in the camp. They were members of a special group aimed at making contact with the very large number of allied prisoner and internees, variously estimated at between 130,000 and 150,000 scattered through 230 camps throughout South East Asia. We were asked to give our name, rank, number and the address of our next of kin to these officers who were like beings from another world – strong, fit, lean men wearing a new type of olive green uniform that we had not seen before. They were the first tangible link with our own people, irrefutable evidence that the war really was over and, for some time, I must admit that I stared at them with a mixture of envy, pride and wonder. They were soon gone however, with a promise of a speedy evacuation and that our next of kin would be informed of our existence. Consequently, our hopes of early departures soon rose again but the days passed without any further news. We heard that Singapore had been occupied by British forces and of the Japanese surrender on September the 2nd.

Soon afterwards some transport aircraft arrived with urgent medical supplies of medicine and food including magazines and newspapers. But the medicine arrived too late for some. A number of men had died since our arrival at the coast. Our impatience was alleviated to the extent that we were now paying daily visits to a nearby market where we bartered our newly issued clothes, cigarettes and blankets for large quantities of duck eggs, duck, fruit, rice and buffalo meat and returning to camp to prepare meals of gargantuan proportions we had dreamt about only a week before. The delights of home – money, clothes, liquor and even sex- all took a second place as we steadily fed ourselves in a relentless effort to assuage the cravings of our bodies for nourishment and vitamins. When we had arrived at this camp, we had all resembled living skeletons with our shaven heads and shrunken faces framing large staring eyes but, after a week or so of our gourmandising, we all began to put on weight even if it was of a flabby, waxy texture. However, with all this sudden invasion of food, there was the inevitable after-effects. Our systems, accustomed to a meagre ill-nourishing diet, now revolted and we were soon all plagued with headaches, nausea and further attacks of dysentery brought on by eating too much fruit. The doctor's warning to us on the need to gradually eat our way back to health had largely gone unheeded and it was only the very few, who had greater reserves of will power, who were able to follow this advice.

While there were those who would not heed the advice of the doctors, there were also many who baulked at camp discipline which the senior officers attempted to maintain in the face of the general euphoria and the removal of the Japanese discipline. The Japanese, however, were still very much in evidence and concerned in various bureaucratic pursuits, compiling lists of prisoners, of the dead and the sick and behaving as if a fairy godmother had waved a magic wand over their heads turning them from swine into well trained lap dogs. A committee of senior officers, British, Dutch and American, ran matters with the Japanese as best they could with the added assistance of some prisoners-of-war now sporting armbands describing themselves as military police. Despite these officers however, once the immediate desires of hunger had to some extent been assuaged, there were many who disappeared into nearby towns and into Batavia in search of drink and women. The British tended to make drink their first priority whereas the Americans reversed the order by seeking women first and then drink. There were a number of British who almost killed themselves by drinking copious draughts of local liquor and Japanese saki and I heard of two Americans who had been knifed to death by some Javanese when they tried to molest their women. There was also a considerable amount of looting. Some men acquired Japanese swords and flags as souvenirs while many of the Dutch colonial troops seemed to have accumulated large kit bags of clothing and shoes. We were also treated to the rather alarming picture one day of an American sergeant, drunk and sated, clutching a flapping white rooster above his head in one hand, firing off a pistol into the air with the other and, simultaneously, trying to dance a jig. He was soon overpowered and unarmed by some of his companions who led him off with soothing words. These were men of the 33rd U.S. Regiment of Artillery who, in the accent of the Bronx, were soon known to us as the 'Dirty Turd.' This commotion and shots from the pistol caused considerable alarm and, at this stage, I began to fear the entire camp would degenerate into an undisciplined rabble in sad contrast to the strong self discipline which we had all accustomed ourselves to.

On the 15th of September, we heard that a Royal Navy cruiser had arrived accompanied by a flotilla of smaller ships. There were delirious scenes the next day as some Royal Marines from HMS Cumberland entered the camp, soon followed by their band playing their jaunty regimental march, 'A Life on the Ocean Wave.' The band had come to cheer us up although this was hardly necessary. And, as we listened to those stirring marches and traditional songs and airs, I finally believed that our long nightmare really had ended and there were very few dry eyes among the British.

A few days later, we were told that we were going to be evacuated to Manila and thence to Britain via Panama or the United States. While many greeted this news with enthusiasm, I was downcast as I had fully expected to travel to Singapore and thence to Britain via India where I would perhaps be able to meet up with my family again. I learned that there were aircraft flying to Batavia from Singapore and Ceylon and presumably were returning empty. Determined to find a passage by this route, I set out to badger as many senior officers as I could. Fortunately one of the reception officers was a RNR Lieutenant and I discovered that he also happened to be an ex-Conway student cadet one term ahead of me. He was more understanding and disclosed that his brother-in-law was a flight lieutenant flying a Dakota aircraft in and out of Singapore. At last I had stumbled into a piece of luck which some people would call the old boy network. Without any qualms, I exploited it to the fullest and, within a few days, just when a large draft of men were leaving to embark for Manila, I was spirited away to the airfield to embark on a Dakota for Singapore.

Before leaving, I said goodbye to Dick Bonser and went in search of Harris and the other Jupiters and Exeters whose number had now been augmented by other naval prisoners. By some miracle, they were all now dressed in smart white shorts and seamen's flannels or vests. They had all put on weight and had a cheerful, expectant look about them. It was a poignant moment as I shook hands with each of them and, finally, with Harris. This was also a difficult moment for me as I looked at this diminutive sailor with an invincible spirit who had, through all those painful years, ungrudgingly responded to every call for assistance with cheerful good humour, never once wavering in the face of the Japanese. There were many things I wanted to say but, because of that ridiculous feeling of embarrassment which seems to register with English men all, "Thanks for everything, Harris," to which he grinned and replied, "The slate's wiped clean, Sir."

They were indeed all men of splendid heart.

Finally on the 18th of September, together with some officers who had managed to wangle a trip on other 'old boy networks', we flew away from that most beautiful of the world's islands which would, alas, always remain in our memories as a land of suffering and hunger.

Within a few hours, we landed at an airfield in Singapore and were immediately taken charge of by the British army and taken to a somewhat seedy looking building with a large sign outside which read RAPWI – Repatriation of Allied Prisoners-of-War and Internees although there were some who, when faced with subsequent long delays swore it really meant – Retain All Prisoners-of-War Indefinitely.

Here we were fed and examined by a battery of medical specialists and issued with a new set of clothing consisting of khaki shirts and slacks. Although the medical examination was thorough, there was not time or facilities to take blood or stool tests and the tropical parasites which infested many of us went undetected until much later in our lives.

As part of our final processing, there was a request that we make statements on our treatment by the Japanese and of our knowledge of any atrocities which would be used in the 'war crimes' investigating teams in an effort to bring those responsible to trial and punishment if necessary. This was greeted with disbelief because the concept of 'war criminals' was, to most of us, an entirely new twist to the game of war. Nevertheless, there was an earnest young Army officer seated behind a desk with an imposing pile of forms with pen poised like some power coercive. As I stood there, my mind went back over all those years which seemed almost a lifetime and I thought of Wright, the Scots flight-sergeant and the three Australians who were bayoneted to death and all those Exeters and Jupiters and others who slowly died from starvation, disease and overwork on Horuko and the three hundred men I helped bury over the side of the Maros Maru during those sixty-seven nightmarish days and of the many senior officers who withstood the worst of it and of that brutal sergeant, Gunzo Mori, his toady Kasiyama and the ineffectual Kasimura. Finally I thought of the ordinary officers and men themselves, those splendid men, Harris and Bunce and the other seamen. I thought of Jim Marsh who was more than a father to me and brave Trevor Latimer. Some men leave no impression on the soul, no matter how often you encounter them in your life but there are those men who touch your life only once and whom you cannot forget for the rest of your days, such men were these. All had endured so much with a spirit which always remained high, cheerful and invincible, never once failing to respond to appeals to their pride or honour of the service, regiment or country. Only very rarely did they flinch or lose their nerve in the face of sudden brutal onslaughts on their person or in the face of slow, grinding starvation, privation, degradation and humiliation. Without their example and their help, I would never have survived and, for one brief moment, I understood the true meaning of 'love my fellowmen and forgiveness of my enemies.'

Suddenly, the Army officer was interrupting my thoughts, "Is there anything you would like to say on this matter?"

"No.....................nothing," and I walked away.

British Military Court

Some years later, I heard that Sergeant Gunzo Mori and his toady Kasiyama were both hanged having been found guilty by a British Military Court of 'brutality and callous indifference to the suffering of hundreds of British and other prisoners which led directly to their deaths.'

The principal evidence against them were the sworn statements of Squadron Leader Pitts and Flight Lieutenant Blackwood, the senior British officer on Horuko and the senior officer on our return journey respectively.

****

We were taken to a requisitioned house in Singapore City which was similar in many ways to the Frances' former residence. It was now converted to a transit officers' mess. We were comfortably looked after and fed by a continuous stream of solicitous orderlies who could not do enough for us. Our chief delight now lay in having clean, white sheets to luxuriate in, soap to bath with and china plates to eat from but, above all, we all treasured the comparative privacy of our quarters after more than three years of existing in public where even the most personal necessities of life were under the constant gaze of our fellows. There were about fifteen other officers in this house who had been collected from various far flung places of South East Asia. There was a gunner captain who had been in charge of one of those huge shore-defence guns of Singapore who had known Hugh Dawson and had also, with a boat load of soldiers and a school atlas, sailed from Singapore to Sumatra, up the Hari River, marched over the mountains until finally reaching Padang on the west coast. Here he had the bitterly frustrating experience of being prevented by the Dutch from signalling to attract the attention of a British cruiser on its final call and, thus, finally falling into Japanese hands. There were others with tales to tell but, as our experiences were all of a similar kind we remained, in general, taciturn and reserved with each other.

One day, I decided to get back into naval uniform and out of the khaki I was wearing. After some setbacks and a considerable amount of talking to a boat's coxswain, I managed to get myself aboard HMS Sussex, a County Class cruiser. I had also been issued with a bush hat with my khaki uniform and, as I stepped aboard and gave the naval salute, there was a look of consternation on the face of the officer of the watch, a young RN sub-lieutenant. After explaining who I was and asking if I could visit the slops for some kit, he couldn't do enough for me. I was soon seated in the gunroom with a glass of beer in my hand and an audience of midshipmen who were inexplicably calling me 'Sir.' I still retained my rank of midshipman but, at the age of twenty-two, I was probably the oldest midshipman in the Royal Navy. Had I survived the war on active service, I supposed I would have been a lieutenant by this time assuming that I would have passed my exams with my journal earning fifty marks.

I felt the warm, enfolding brotherhood of the Royal Navy once again for more than an hour. None of them would hear of me buying kit from the slops and, within no time, articles of uniform were being thrust upon me including a cap which fitted perfectly.

Soon afterwards, I was introduced to the Commander and invited to stay on board for lunch with some other ex-prisoner naval officers who had also come on board. I finally left in an alcoholic haze that afternoon carrying a kit bag with additional shorts, shirts and stockings. The whole experience had been a homecoming. It was this style – a Nelsonic love for one another, a self-protective fraternity and sense of membership of an exclusive club where one became a paid up member for life, linked up forever by comradeship to all other naval men which had sustained us over all these years. As naval men we had always stuck fiercely to our own small group but never at odds nor unready to help others in need but there were times when we decried the attempts of certain Army and RAF officers when they tried to impose some of their sillier pompous and irrelevant military ways upon us.

Singapore was slowly emerging from a bad nightmare. The people wore a stunned look despite the recent jubilation associated with liberation. The streets were overgrown and untidy with many buildings destroyed or damaged by bombing. I found a brief message for me when I returned to the mess in response to a cable I had sent upon my arrival in Singapore. It was from my mother in Delhi saying, 'Much relieved. Looking forward to seeing you again soon.' They were the only words I had heard from my family for over three years. While we were in Java, the Japanese had issued us with small pre-printed cards and we were told to fill these in with a brief message but I had learned that these were never received probably because they were never sent. I also learned some time later that I had been posted as missing after the sinking of the Exeter. About six months later, my parents received a further communication from the Admiralty saying that it was known that a large number of the survivors from the Exeter had fallen into Japanese hands but, regretfully, I was not among them – 'it is now presumed that your son lost his life when the ship in which he was serving was sunk by enemy action.'

Some time in 1944, they were informed that it had now been ascertained that I was alive and in a prison camp in Java even if I was, in fact, in Horuko at the time.

I now wanted to get to India to see my family again but I soon found out that I was to join a transport ship sailing for England simultaneously with the news that I had been promoted to sub-lieutenant, obviously an aged midshipman was becoming a bit of an embarrassment to the Navy. Determined somehow to get myself diverted to India en route to England, I made my way to the RAPWI offices and, after a whole day of waiting and badgering various officers who were disinclined to change well laid plans, the navy came to my rescue once again when I found a sympathetic Lieutenant-commander who seemed to have a wide range of contacts. I was at the airfield within days and boarding a Dakota armed with a warrant giving me Priority 2 which was to subsequently raise some eyebrows at the other end when it was explained to me that this level of priority was reserved for the Commander in Chief and Staff only. Such being the case, I could only wonder who would be afforded Priority 1 but I was, nevertheless, impressed with the naval officer's influence.

We were soon airborne and, as we circled, I glimpsed for the last time, the naval base looking much as it did in 1942. We stopped briefly in Rangoon in a heavy downpour and then landed at Dum Dum airfield near Calcutta where I was, once again, given ex prisoner-of-war reception. This was continued when I was taken to Fort Belvedere, the former residence of the Lieutenant Governor of Bengal and now partly given over to the reception of those such as myself. Despite my protestations of having gone through all this in Singapore I, nevertheless, submitted to further medical examinations and interrogation but declined, once again, to make a statement of war crimes. There was a large group of British ladies administering to our welfare and I was soon being looked after with the greatest kindness. One of them tried to get my parents on the telephone in New Delhi without success but sent a message to say when I would be arriving. The Howrah-Delhi mail was crowded but I managed to get a seat and settled down with a pleasurable glow of anticipation. Twenty-four hours later, the train pulled in to Old Delhi station.

It was nearly fourteen years since I had last seen Delhi and it was all so compellingly familiar. While old Delhi station was much the same, things had changed greatly since then. There were soldiers everywhere – British and Indian – and armed sentries at the barriers keeping back the floods of luggage coolies who usually smothered the travellers as they alighted although a favoured few were let through. I handed my valise to one of them and said, 'Taxi,' and walked past a barrier and a large notice which said RTO – All Military Personnel will report here.

Deciding I was naval rather than military, I ignored this injunction and marched on almost bumping into my boyishly handsome and now a Pilot Officer in the RAF, brother hurrying through the entrance to meet me. After a period of only half recognition and a brief exchange, we fought our way to a taxi through a milling throng and were soon rumbling down Queens Road.

My brother began to talk and then, unbelievably I was listening as he told me about my father's death a year ago in Assam. This was a severe and unexpected shock and I was completely stunned. As we turned right at the Fort with the Lahore Gate looking down the street of Silversmiths –the Chandi Chawk – with the Jurma Musjid soaring above the filthy shacks and festering bazaars and the Golden Mosque on the left with a glimpse of the Jurma in the distance, I saw the India which had also fascinated my father; the milling sea of black, brown and yellow faces and the sharp smell of dust, spices and marigold. As the taxi hooted and pushed its way through a maelstrom of cars, tongas, army lorries and buses, I thought of that day at Mount Lavinia in Ceylon over three years ago and great sadness and utter despair came over me.

"When was it?" I asked

"21st of March, 44, more than eighteen months now," he said.

I tried to remember where I was on that day – the moment he died – but the date was meaningless and lost in the blur of Horuko where one day was like the rest and where a man's death was only briefly mourned. A great sadness and utter despair came over me. No tears came to my eyes for I now felt incapable of further grief.

It was a sad homecoming for my presence only served to re-open my mother's healed wounds of grief. After nearly a fortnight of playing the dutiful son during the day and joining in the round of parties with my brother in the evening, it all began to pall. The parties were invariably raucous, a combination of mess nights in private houses with young girls, not a few of whom were Wack-eyes or Women's Army Corps (Indian) some of whom being delightfully chee-chee. The war had brought many changes and the old class and racial barriers of India were now being broken down in a frenetic, temporary and shifting society fed on the exuberance of victory. Many of my brother's friends were, like him, newly commissioned and recently arrived in India but, unlike him, tended to be overbearing and gauche. At one party, a drunken flying officer suddenly grabbed me by the throat and said, "How's our sailor hero then, been everywhere haven't you and poor old Smithy here never did see a Jap." At that point I decided it was time I left Delhi, even if it meant breaking off a very promising encounter with a delicious looking young Wack-eye.

I left Delhi the next day for Rawalpindi after an uncomfortable half hour with an overweight red-faced major, the Railway Transport Officer in Delhi who refused to recognise my presence because I had not reported my arrival as ordered to do so. When I said that military did not include naval, he said, "Don't be clever, Sir. The railway is under military jurisdiction and military means the army, the airforce and even the bloody navy." Without his authorisation, I couldn't buy a ticket even if I was travelling privately on leave. However, within two days, I was being driven at hair-raising speed by a young, wild looking Pathan corporal across the Pir Panjit range and descending into the Vale of Kashmir in a jeep kindly provided by a former army friend of my father's who was now stationed in Rawalpindi.

Winter was in the air and it was cold, in fact rather too late in the year for a comfortable visit to Kashmir. But, as we descended the Barramula road along the fast flowing Jhelum River towards Srinagar, through straight avenues of poplars planted by the Moghuls, with the brown flanking fields against a backdrop of the Himalayas to the north with the snows only briefly exposed through the cloud, it became steadily warmer. It was a captivating scene and when finally installed in the warm, cosy comfort of a house-boat lent to me by another friend - this time, one of my mother's – and tended by two solicitous servants, I felt at peace.

I would sleep every day, rise to a hot bath and a large breakfast of yoghurt, cheese, eggs, kedgeree and roti with innumerable cups of tea. When it rained, as it frequently did, I would remain on board reading from the large library of old books and outdated magazines. When it was clear, I would take a shikari across the lake to Srinagar and wander through the bazaar with its narrow, obscure lanes inhabited by a polyglot confusion of people – many dressed in thick, sheepskins or brown woollen cloaks under which they carried a kangri – a brass brazier of warm charcoals as a personal heating system. In evidence were also a number of convalescing servicemen with the tempting sounds of their nightly revels sometimes floating across the waters of Lake Dal. One day, perhaps propelled for my quest for continuity, I climbed the steep pinnacle hill which overlooks the lake and town to the small temple of Siva at its summit, named after Sankaracharya who came to Srinagar from India over a thousand years ago to revive Hinduism which had been eclipsed by Buddhism. I had climbed this same hill many years ago with my parents, having had to be carried the last stages on my father's back.

Now that I was finally alone with myself, I was strangely lonely. At first I was terrified. The thought of emerging from the house-boat filled me with dread but, as the days passed, I began to regain some balance and composure and my loneliness became a secure solitude. After years of living in close confinement with others, the jade light of the valley, the silence of the lake and the mountains, the gentle, lapping, paddling of the shikara-wallah and speaking only to those whom I chose to speak to, acted like a sensuous balm to my still raw nerves. Then, suddenly, after breakfast one day, I knew it was time to go back and start a new life.

****

The years were not easy for the many thousands of ex-prisoners of the Japanese. Many, in attempting to make a new life, were plagued with the after effects of amoebic dysentry and beri-beri as well as the unexpected effects of benign types of malaria, hook-worm, liver fluke and other debilitating tropical diseases. The strain of overwork and the effects of malnutrition in their youth served to weaken constitutions causing many to die, sometimes inexplicably, in their middle years of life, and it was not only these physical effects. The mental scars made many men difficult to live with, an unreasonable impatience with the petty preoccupations of others; a strong compulsion for frequent changes of occupation and scenery with an obsession over minor details were common and with stability and emotional maturity being long delayed.

There were those, however, who were able to shrug off the whole experience without apparent ill-effect but, on the other hand, there were those who, as prisoners, were indestructable, who slowly declined over the years as though all their reserves had been consumed in one bright flare. Such a man was Harris.

In 1959, whilst on leave from Africa, I lived for some time at Blackheath and, one evening, as I sat in the Admiral Blake, the pub at the gates to Greenwich Naval College where I had spent many a happy evening twenty years before, I happened to look up to see Harris mirrored in the wall opposite and staring intently at me, looking as though he had seen a ghost. I learned that he had left the navy soon after the war, joined the post-office, had married and now lived in nearby Lewisham. Taking him up on his invitation to supper, I called round at the house one evening later in the week. His wife was a small, dumpy, over sympathetic woman who also proved to be an excellent cook. It was then that I noticed Harris's resigned and lethargic manner and, in an effort to keep the conversation going, I told him something of my life in Africa. This failed to elicit a response. We hardly spoke of Horuko or that infamous journey back to Java, nor of all those years together. I realised that the only bond between us was one that he wanted to forget.

Three years later, on leave again and on a sudden impulse, I called at his house. A strange woman answered the door.

"No, the Harrises no longer live here," she told me. "He died you know, seems he was a prisoner of the Japs or something during the war, had a bad time of it and never got over it."

After all this time I remain equivocal about the Japanese. There is much to admire in their character, their appreciation of simple, startlingly effective design, grace and beauty, their industriousness, obedience, cleanliness and their high sense of filial honour and duty. There are those who see the barbaric excesses of their behaviour during that period to be a manifestation of cultural traits developed over centuries and founded upon a corrupted form of Shintoism and the precepts of 'bushido.' This, I believe, to be only partly true and in consent of the prevalent notion of moral relativism and a reluctance to admit that absolute evil can and does exist. This makes it especially difficult for some to accept the fact that Japanese behaviour during the war and, indeed, the recent and continuing genocidal experience of Indonesia, China, Biafra, Uganda and Cambodia, is something far worse than abherrant behaviour. Rather, I believe it to be the deadly consequence of an atheist egocentric system of values enforced by fallible human beings with total power, who believe that morality is whatever the powerful define it to be, knowing always that any totalitarian system seems to bring out the worst aspects of a nation's character. Today we see a similar deadly consequence of the different totalitarian creeds of Marxism and Maoism steadily gaining ground throughout the Far East and Africa and only diluted in Europe by what the present day prophet, Solzhenitsyn has called 'the great reserves of mercy and sacrifice' from a Christian tradition. Sadly, one can only agree with Hegel that 'peoples and governments never have learned anything from history, nor acted on principles deduced from it.'

The Japanese onslaught on Asia in the third and fourth decades of the twentieth century was perhaps as much an expression of the need for living space and resources as it was an act of revenge upon Europeans and Americans, who had, up to that time, insensitively dominated the East and repeatedly humiliated the delicate pride of its peoples even if much of it was benign and unintended. It was, in its way, the final reaction against the commercial, evangelistic and political aggression of the West which saw its beginnings in the outburst of rage against the British in 1857. The atrocities inflicted upon those Europeans, Americans and Chinese who fell into Japanese hands in Hong Kong, Singapore, Manila and elsewhere equalled those revengeful barbarities, at the hands of the Indians only eighty years before. Certainly all Japanese acts against European prisoners were dictated by a desire to humiliate and degrade, particularly so when an audience of the local population was present.

Although the obliteration of Hiroshima and Nagasaki in 1945 stunned the Japanese into surrender, halted the increasing tempo of retribution by the Allies and, undoubtedly saved all prisoners-of-war from either a slow death from starvation and disease or by massacre, it did little to restore the West's position in the East in the post-war years. Indeed, it may well be history's verdict that despite her ultimate defeat in the field, Japan won a lasting victory in that part of the world. What Japan achieved in 1941-5 was the hastening of the decline of the West in Asia. The stigma of defeat in 1942 hung heavily on the British, French and Dutch when they endeavoured to re-establish their hegemony in 1945 in the face of an indigenous development of national self-consciousness and corresponding political movements which were directed above all against the re-imposition of colonial rule.

The surrender signatories aboard the Missouri

Apart from some final, bloody and sometimes ignominious death throes, the Europeans were soon forced to relinquish their attempts to re-impose their rule and by the 1960s had virtually abdicated. The United States, however, having perhaps learned little from the immediate past and even less of the long pendulum swings of history, was then reluctantly drawn into this vacuum. After two more decades of further bloody contest and suffering, which was nothing more than a post-script to an era of Western dominance which had lasted for some five hundred years, the United States finally conceded defeat and withdrew. During this closing act, Japan recanted and, under the benevolence of the United States intent on remaking Japan in her own image, assiduously worked to establish herself as the premier economic power of the East and to become, by the mid 1970s, one of the world's major industrial powers. It is perhaps with some chagrin that the United States now see the decline of her currency in the face of the Japanese competition and protection on the world's markets which has placed Japan well beyond any aims she may have entertained in the 1930s. History is indeed full of irony.

****

Thirty years later, I returned to the Far East and stopped over in Bangkok and Singapore on my way back to New Zealand to attend a happy family occasion. Whilst in Bangkok, I decided to visit Kachanaburu, the site of the bridge on the River Kwai and the collective cemetery and memorial to the 17,000 prisoners-of-war who died there on the Siam-Burma railway under conditions similar to those which we endured in Horuko. However I did not go because when the tourist bus arrived at our hotel, it contained a large party of Japanese tourists heavily laden with cameras, all hissing and nodding rapidly among themselves. I turned away and cancelled my trip. I left for Singapore the same day.

Raffles Hotel and the padang were still there, the former now seedy and run down, rather like an aged, painted lady fingering her ill-gotten pearls in apprehensive glances over her shoulder at the arrival of younger, brasher and more brazen competitors. The new city-state of Singapore was no longer that staid epitomy of the Raj but now a more lively, vulgar city humming with a new Asian spirit. The British had long since departed but their imposing public buildings remained like the ruins of some past civilisation and managing, somehow, to look disdainful at the sudden influx of nouveau riche into what was once their own private and exclusive market place. I made a short pilgrimage to Kranji war cemetery and there, set apart from the long meticulous lines of white engraved headstones, those silent memorials to wasted lives, found a dozen or so graves of men from the Prince of Wales and the Repulse who died on that night we returned to this island so long ago. Later, back in Singapore and in the tall, white, serene Anglican cathedral, I found a plaque to the memory of Admiral Sir Tom Spencer Vaughan Phillips KCB, two other officers and to all who had died on HMS Prince of Wales and Repulse, 10th of December 1941. Flanking it was another plaque to the memory of those Australian nursing sisters who were brutally murdered by the Japanese in Singapore and on Banka Island in February 1942 – the word 'murder' shockingly frank in an age grown used to euphemisms used to describe the continuing and dismal process of man's inhumanity to man.

Upon my return, I flew from New Zealand to Sydney and thence to Hong Kong. We were joined by a large party of Japanese at Sydney, all with small identification badges and obviously on a works-organised tour. This time, there was no avoiding them as they occupied the front half of the aircraft and kept up a boisterous chatter amongst themselves. At Darwin, a young Australian couple joined the flight and sat next to me on the aisle and soon the husband was talking to me. He was tall, red-headed with a long, rangy, characteristic Australian face and he told me that this was the first time he had ever flown, that he was a driller from Mount Isa and he and his bride were on their way to Hong Kong for their honeymoon. As the aircraft flew on over the Banda Sea, he looked past me through the window and drew my attention to some islands below us. I looked down and there, suddenly, was the island of Ambiona and, in the haze to the east, Horuko. The town of Ambon, the houses glinting white in the late afternoon sun against the green backcloth of the island looked serene and peaceful. I told the young man that the larger island was Ambiona and the island further to the east was Horuko.

"You been there?" he asked obviously impressed with my geographical knowledge.

"Yes," I said, "a long time ago."

"Looks a nice place."

"Yes," I said, "I suppose it is."

British and American flags being hoisted on Fort No2 Tokyo Bay 29ᵗʰ August 1945. Taken by a member of the British Landing Force

Inspecting a range finder on Tokyo Bay Fort No2

205

Mt Fujiyama taken from Sagami Bay 1945

Japanese suicide bomber hitting HMS Victorious at sea – Okubawa April 1945

In front of the Imperial Palace Tokyo
on the 6th Anniversary of the outbreak of War, 3rd Sept 1945

9th Aug 1945
Fleet returning from bombardment of Kamaishi Japan.
Also day of Atomic bomb dropped on Hiroshima.
Destroyer re-fuelling alongside KGV in background.